GREAT CAMP
SAGAMORE

GREAT CAMP SAGAMORE

THE VANDERBILTS' ADIRONDACK RETREAT

BEVERLY BRIDGER

Foreword by Alfred Vanderbilt III

THE
History
PRESS

Published by The History Press
Charleston, SC 29403
www.historypress.net

Cover images and all color images by Davescranton.com, © Adirondack IMAGES
Photography.
Vanderbilt family photos included by permission of Alfred G. Vanderbilt. Collins photos
from Sagamore archives with thanks.
Unless otherwise noted, images appear courtesy of the Sagamore collection.
Letters in Appendix III appear courtesy of the Collins family.
With gratitude, the author recognizes Anne R. Bertholf for her generous assistance with
many textual details.

First published 2012

Manufactured in the United States

ISBN 978.1.60949.589.3

Library of Congress CIP data applied for.

To Barbara Glaser,
founder, philanthropist and friend
who won't take credit for saving Sagamore, but who must, in her natural good
grace, allow me to give it to her.

And to Leigh, Drew and Michael, who have lived and loved Sagamore with me.

Road marker. *Photo from "Three Miles to Sagamore," a Vanderbilt family photo album from the 1940s donated to Sagamore by Alfred G. Vanderbilt. Photographer: Bert Clark Thayer.*

Contents

Inspired by the American arts and crafts movement, Sagamore is a standing monument to its artisans. They used the materials of the land and in doing so honored for us all our connection to nature.

In New York City, Mrs. Astor might have said to Mrs. Vanderbilt in polite conversation, "Tell me, my dear, when are you vacating to your Adirondack camp this year?" The reply from Mrs. Vanderbilt might have been, "We plan to vacate by July 10th." The "vacation" was invented in the Adirondacks.

Foreword

It was like Brigadoon, the legendary village that appeared out of the mists only once every seven years, just to disappear again. The people who lived in the village aged just one year of seven. And everyone was happy all the time. That's how I remember Sagamore.

We never called it a "Great Camp." Usually, we just said camp, or Sagamore. "Are you coming up to camp? We hope you will."

My grandfather, the first Alfred Gwynne Vanderbilt, bought Sagamore from William West Durant in 1901. The Vanderbilts were one of early America's success stories. Cornelius Vanderbilt ("the Commodore") made the family's fortune in shipping before the Civil War. By his sixties, he was the richest man in America. At about seventy years of age, he sold all his shipping interests and began buying the independent railroads that were springing up in and around New York City. He unified them, built Grand Central Terminal and named the Vanderbilt railroad the New York Central.

He left everything to his oldest son, William Henry Vanderbilt. By the time William died in 1885, the fortune had become the largest in the world. Cornelius Vanderbilt II, my grandfather's father, was next in line, and when he died in 1899, Alfred became his primary heir.

For Alfred, who was newly married and just twenty-four years old, Sagamore was a key part of an extraordinary life.

His parents' generation had built some of the largest mansions in the country, and he had grown up in a 154-room Loire Valley–style chateau that took up the entire west side of Fifth Avenue between Fifty-seventh and Fifty-eighth Streets. His cousin Consuelo Vanderbilt had married the Duke of Marlborough and was overseeing the restoration of Blenheim Palace. His sister, Gladys, married Count Szechenyi of Hungary.

Building mansions, however, seems to have been exactly what Alfred Vanderbilt did not want to do. He preferred an active life, a country life, and spent as much time outdoors as he could. His main residence was an agrarian estate in Portsmouth, Rhode Island, called Oakland Farms. Located near Newport, Rhode Island, the summer seat of the family, Oakland made it convenient for Alfred to visit his mother, Mrs. Cornelius Vanderbilt II, at the Breakers, her seventy-room summer palazzo.

He solved the problem of a New York residence in 1907 by becoming the first guest to sign the register at the Plaza Hotel, where he maintained a nine-room suite and later, in 1912, built a hotel of his own: the Vanderbilt, at Thirty-fourth Street and Park Avenue. He kept apartments and town houses in London and Paris and estates in the countryside around them. In 1909, he commissioned the largest houseboat in England (it was larger than the royal family's) so his family could watch the regatta.

He became a jet-setter before commercial aviation existed, traveling almost constantly, going to Europe as many as ten times a year when an ocean crossing could take as long as two weeks. Once, he traveled by ocean liner with one hundred horses, to drive his coach between London and Brighton. For Alfred, a camp in the Adirondacks was a perfect complement to his evolving lifestyle.

In 1909, he divorced his first wife and two years later married Margaret Emerson McKim, daughter of Dr. Isaac Emerson of Baltimore, the inventor of Bromo-Seltzer. Young and vivacious, Margaret was the apple of her father's eye, and when she and my grandfather met for the first time at the Plaza Hotel in the winter of 1908, they fell in love. The newlyweds shared an equal passion for outdoor life.

It's not hard to imagine Alfred bringing Margaret to camp for the first time. They would have been thirty-one and twenty-six years old; he was handsome, and she was beautiful. They would have taken his private rail car, the Wayfarer, traveling the long hours through the countryside from Grand Central Terminal.

Finally nearing the end of the two-day trip, they would have come through the sweet pines at dusk. As the horse-drawn carriages drew near to camp, fires and Roman candles were lit all along the miles of road. It was part of a tradition, a drum roll of sorts, to alert people in camp that visitors were arriving and to tell the visitors that they were about to experience something extraordinary.

As the fires were lit, the woods would have come alive from the sound of the coach wheels, harnesses and the horses' hooves striking gravel. Trail guides would have waved to the guests from their positions along the road. And then, as the carriages slowed approaching the entrance to camp, the travelers would have felt the deep, healing peace of the Adirondacks.

And then as they came over the rise, Sagamore appeared like a jewel—those extraordinary wooden buildings set perfectly on the glittering lake with a manicured croquet lawn as its centerpiece. The lights in the Main Lodge, dining hall and cabins would have sent a warm glow across the compound as the smell of wood fires and delicious food wafted up from the kitchen. And at last, as the horses came to a rest, the weary travelers would know they had found heaven.

I was a small child when I came to camp. What I remember best are the deer walking through the compound to eat from our hands like pets, the sunlight on the Main Lodge, the mists every morning on the lake and the atmosphere of fun and enthusiasm that pervaded Sagamore at all times. It was an honor to be in camp. I knew that even then.

In the eyes of the larger world, the Vanderbilts' camp was a secret. For decades, the press hounded the family, but Sagamore was one place reporters could not go. Grandfather and Grandmother felt safe bringing their family and closest friends. My father and mother felt the same way.

A typical letter from my grandfather's secretary to Mr. Collins, the indispensable manager of Sagamore, would alert him that Mr. and Mrs. Vanderbilt would be arriving in a few days with a group of sixteen or twenty. That meant that bedrooms, food and service and activities for the guests and the family had to be ready and all had to be flawless. It was: service at Sagamore was far better than at any five-star hotel. The family not only loved to spend August in camp, but also Christmases at Sagamore were frequent, as were visits in the fall and spring.

In May 1915, my grandfather embarked on what he thought was just another trip to London. He sailed aboard *Lusitania* when it was torpedoed by a German U-boat. After the explosion, the ship went down in eighteen minutes, about the time it takes to finish a dry martini. The only outdoor sport my grandfather could not do was swim. But he gave his life preserver to a panicked woman and hunted through the ship for children, putting many into lifeboats himself. Then, thirty-seven years old, a vision of calm bravery, he stood by the railing waiting for the end.

After her husband's death, Grandmother decided to keep Sagamore. Grandfather had loved it dearly; it had quite possibly been his favorite place in the world. And Margaret kept it as a tribute to him, because she had come to love it too.

For several years, her guest lists focused on her late husband's family and friends, especially during the long summer polio outbreaks in the Northeast. Eventually, however, her guests became more diverse. She loved to be with interesting people, and she loved to be outdoors. So, in the deep of the Adirondack woods, far from spying eyes, she brought together the most interesting people she could find in the world: artists and writers, scientists and statesmen, actors and musicians.

Notable guests at camp included General George Marshall, who won the Nobel Prize the year he visited camp for his reorganization of postwar Europe. Richard Rogers, the great Broadway songwriter and producer, came often. Howard Hughes, the aviation pioneer and motion picture tycoon, and movie stars like Gary Cooper, Clifton Webb and Gene Tierney also visited. Like an invitation to the White House, being asked to visit Sagamore was an opportunity not to be missed.

Perhaps Grandmother's most notorious visitor was Madame Chiang Kai-Chek, wife of the imperial emperor of China. Madame Chiang's visit, while social, was of international importance. To make room for her, Grandmother vacated her own camp. Madame Chiang Kai-Chek came with twenty-five personal maids. Three maids were always assigned just to watch Madame Chiang's bedsheets—even while she was out of the room. If even a breath of wind ruffled the sheets, they had to be changed immediately!

Despite Margaret Emerson's social position, she was never a slave to convention and always loved being outdoors. She was a crack shot, and while traveling through the American West, she shot and killed a grizzly bear. She also shot an intruder in her house in Reno. She traveled worldwide and hunted rhinoceros, hippopotami, lions and tigers in Africa. She was a woman unafraid of her own life.

One night at camp, a champion boxer became interested in one of the young women on staff. The girl explained to him that she was engaged to one of Sagamore's trail guides, but the fighter would not leave her alone. Finally, after many warnings, the girl's fiancé knocked the boxer unconscious, using the butt of his rifle.

The next morning, Margaret fired the guide on the spot and apologized to her hung-over guest. As soon as he was gone from camp, she summoned the guide and rehired him. She knew that if one of her guests needed to be separated from his consciousness, no one would be a better judge of the situation than a member of her staff. She cared deeply about the camp families for as long as she lived.

One day, she called her sons together. "When I'm gone," she said, "will you keep Sagamore Lodge up? Will you maintain it the way I have, the way it should be?"

She had sustained the camp and cared for its families for nearly half a decade, through her youth, the death of her first husband, the birth of two sons and a daughter, three subsequent marriages and two world wars, but now, as she neared seventy, an illness was gaining ground on her. When Alfred and George looked at each other silently, she knew the family's time as stewards of Sagamore had come to an end.

Once the decision was made, she did everything that she could to see that camp and the camp families were cared for and that Sagamore itself would be preserved, if such a thing were possible. It wasn't. Sagamore passed though several owners, deteriorating under each, until it was finally rescued by a determined group of preservationists led by Barbara Glaser and Beverly Bridger, founders of the Sagamore Institute.

Early visitors to Sagmore arrived by horse-drawn carriage.

I want to applaud the heroic job they have done maintaining and preserving what was left of the camp when they got it. The outbuildings, the fields and farm, the flower gardens and greenhouses, vegetable gardens, softball fields and toboggan run and so much more have all given way to time and the inexorable march of the forest. Like Brigadoon, much of Sagamore has disappeared.

But even now, in its slightly diminished state, its magnificence is hardly dimmed. And after the long, sweet drive through the darkening woods, whenever I come over the rise and see those beautiful buildings perched on that perfect lake, I know what it must have been like for Alfred and Margaret when they came to see it together for the first time.

It was like seeing Brigadoon rise from the mists. Like coming to heaven.

—Alfred G. Vanderbilt III

Margaret

M argaret Emerson McKim Vanderbilt Baker Amory Emerson was a devoted steward of Sagamore from 1911, when she married Alfred G. Vanderbilt (owner of Sagamore since 1901), until 1954, when she gifted her beloved camp to Syracuse University. Born at the outset of the Gilded Age in 1884, she enjoyed storybook advantages available to her because of the affluence of her father. Margaret married four times, once to the wealthiest young man in America. She was an honored member of high society; a volunteer in the war efforts; a divorced, widowed and liberated-before-her-time woman; an excommunicated and reinstated Catholic; the head of the Red Cross in the Pacific in World War II; a mother and grandmother; a sportswoman; and the hostess of Sagamore Lodge for over forty years.

Her father, Isaac Emerson, invented Bromo-Seltzer, one of several formulas he had concocted for Margaret's headache-plagued mother. Isaac held the patent and manufactured this highly profitable medication in Baltimore, where Margaret grew up learning the charms and social graces of the South.

In 1902, she married Smith Hollis McKim, a physician of good family but no fortune, who had been, according to the *New York Times,* a guest aboard her father's yacht on a cruise around the world. They were touted as one of high society's most popular couples in Baltimore, New York City, Palm Beach, Newport and South Carolina. When Mrs. William Astor died, the society columnists elected Margaret her successor to lead the

Four Hundred, the crème de la crème of society (and, as a practical measure, the number of people who could dance in Mrs. Astor's ballroom).

After eight years of marriage, Isaac took his daughter Margaret to Reno to obtain a divorce from the brutal McKim. It was a sensational case. Margaret claimed he beat her when he was drunk; he countersued, claiming alienation of affection. Isaac Emerson settled with McKim out of court. Margaret was excommunicated from the Catholic Church, a punishment that pained her deeply.

Margaret Emerson McKim Vanderbilt Baker Amory Emerson.

Her next husband was Alfred G. Vanderbilt. They had two sons, Alfred G. and George W., before Alfred Sr. died heroically on the *Lusitania*. Her third husband was Raymond T. Baker, father of daughter Gloria (called Mimi). Margaret had a brief fourth marriage, and after that divorce, she reclaimed her maiden name, Margaret Emerson.

Divorce among the leaders of society was not taken lightly. Teddy Roosevelt, premier example of the Gilded Age gentleman, was very vocal about divorce among his social class. He did not approve of breaking the sacred bond of marriage and felt that his peers should set a superior example. In spite of his opinion, divorces did occur at the turn of that century. Some would credit the Industrial Age and the movement to the cities for this rent in the social fabric.

The Gilded Age

*

Sagamore is a product of its era. Mark Twain dubbed it the Gilded Age, that time in our history after the Civil War and up to the beginning of the First World War when a few people made vast amounts of money. Do not mistake the beginnings of World War I as the impetus for the demise of the era: it was the income tax (Article XVI of the Constitution) in February 1913 that began to rein in the extravagance. "Gilded" was the term Twain used to describe the conspicuous displays of wealth centered in New York City, a metropolis untouched by the ravages of the Civil War, thus able to grow and expand while other communities could only garner their forces for an arduous reconstruction. Huge mansions covering entire city blocks were built, grand hotels with plumbing opened and high society was in full bloom. History also recognizes this era as the Industrial Revolution and the wealthy class as the captains of industry or robber barons.

Except for J.P. Morgan, these men were not formally educated. They had grown up in rural America and discovered, invented or improved a way to make something or to provide a service that earned them millions. Because our nation had not yet had time to develop an American culture, having been distracted by the need to settle the nation and fight various wars, the newly wealthy turned their eyes to Europe to see what the aristocracy was doing. They discovered that the aristocracy went to college, read in its leisure time, had paintings on the walls of the castles and enjoyed a social season. Soon, Vanderbilt and Stanford endowed colleges, Carnegie donated libraries until 2,500 small towns could boast them and J.P. Morgan hired a

An interior room for guests of Sagamore, strikingly different than the meager accommodations for workers.

woman to do nothing but buy art work, amassing so many paintings that, at his death, the Metropolitan Museum of Art grew from his collection. The social season was laden with balls and theater openings. To cope with the heat of summer, high society built Newport's ninety-room "cottages" to go to the beach and Adirondack "camps" to escape to the woods for wilderness recreation opportunities new to the young United States.

The designation "Great Camp" is a relatively new term coined in the 1980s. By definition, Great Camps were built for a single family (in our case the Vanderbilts). They had their own water sources. They generally imitated European architecture but were built of indigenous all-natural materials. The separate buildings of a Great Camp each had separate functions, and such camps were built in remote locations. The most significant determining feature, however, is that they were meant to be self-sustaining. They have a farm site and gardens. Their workers' complex or village housed people who made their livings in concert with nature, on and from the land, and from the wages paid to them for building and maintaining the camp year-round, even though the family would only use it a few weeks.

The Vanderbilts' Adirondack Retreat

Some Sagamore visitors, having seen the Biltmore, the Breakers or Marble House, tell us that Sagamore just doesn't measure up to the other Vanderbilt estates. Why, they wonder, is it called a "Great Camp?" We ask them how they go camping—in a tent, an RV, a pop-up trailer? The Vanderbilts camped in sixty buildings on a private lake in the midst of 1,526 acres. The contrast is obvious. Sagamore is the prototypical Great Camp of the Gilded Age.

Twain's metaphor for this era was well selected. "Gilding" was the process of painting a paper-thin layer of gold over a plaster of Paris base or one of a lesser metal base to make it glitter. As the American industrial era emerged, high society produced a thin layer of glittering dissipation over the myriad social problems of the times. Consider: emulating European royalty, those in high society had apparently forgotten George Washington's stand against being elected president-for-life because it smacked of monarchy, the very system America had just overthrown.

A cursory look through the Gilded Age headlines of the *New York Times* reveals not just the lifestyles of Margaret's peers in high society but also the severe suffering of the working class. Hunger, homelessness, child labor, slums, unemployment and wretchedness of all descriptions led the way to strikes, riots and monopoly-breaking lawsuits as a young and spirited nation sought solutions to its social problems. The great division between rich and poor spawned the great equalizer, the income tax, which paved the way for a strong middle class.

The dining hall complex and main lodge from the lake. *Photo from "Three Miles to Sagamore," a Vanderbilt family photo album from the 1940s donated to Sagamore by Alfred G. Vanderbilt. Photographer: Bert Clark Thayer.*

The barn and other service buildings in the caretaker's complex. *Photo from "Three Miles to Sagamore," a Vanderbilt family photo album from the 1940s donated to Sagamore by Alfred G. Vanderbilt. Photographer: Bert Clark Thayer.*

The architectural styles at Margaret's beloved Sagamore mirror these same divisions. The workers were separated from the guests by their own entrance to camp and by a tall garden fence in the center of camp that provided a picturesque physical barrier. Buildings for the workers were functional structures, the red board-and-batten style commonly used for farm structures. Buildings for the guests were bark-covered fantasies, rustic and recreational. Sagamore, as all great estates of its era, operated with a social distinction and division that is no longer generally observed. Margaret grew up when it was not uncommon to find wealthy members of society who believed they were "chosen," and as they set out to conquer the frontier by gun and by railroad, they thought of it as Manifest Destiny. Her father, Alfred's grandfather, and their fellow captains of industry all recognized and lived by these values.

The Adirondack Vacation

L ike other Gilded Agers, Margaret enjoyed summers in the Adirondack Park, a vast state park larger than the combined acreage of all the national parks in the contiguous forty-eight states. Late to be explored, the Adirondack region was bypassed by the victorious soldiers of the Revolutionary War who were given the opportunity to take the equivalent of "forty acres and a mule." Instead, they chose more hospitable land in Ohio and farther west. Not until the late nineteenth century was this region made a park, established in 1892 as a response to the outcry of New York City residents who were horrified to see the Hudson River run with mud from clear-cut deforestation practices. It quickly became the destination for the most adventuresome of the wealthy.

New York City residents realized that to save their water, they had to begin by saving the land around their future water sources. From this realization grew a movement, illustrated magnificently by the Hudson River School of painters, which sought to protect lands in the Adirondacks and the more immediately needed Catskills. The clear-cutting that harvested the logs to be driven to market south on the Hudson River and drove the railroads north to bring men and supplies to the forest also eroded the land. To exacerbate matters, sparks from locomotive smokestacks often ignited the slash piles left by the timber extractors and burned whatever was left standing. Runoff from Adirondack spring thaws and summer thunderstorms darkened the Hudson River waters and alerted people to a land abuse problem.

Based on Verplank Colvin's survey of the Adirondack forest, luminaries like Teddy Roosevelt joined to establish the park. Learning of William West Durant's developments around Raquette Lake and Paul Smith's attempts to promote tourism by establishing resort facilities in the mountains, wealthy New Yorkers headed north to the newly fashionable park, motivated by curiosity, social pressure and a desire to participate in and demonstrate man's dominion over nature.

Years before she became an owner of Sagamore, Margaret had visited the Adirondacks—as a guest of Mr. and Mrs. Reginald Vanderbilt, the brother and sister-in-law of her future husband, Alfred. She was Mrs. McKim when, with her husband, she was invited to Long Lake, the home of William K. Vanderbilt, uncle of Reginald and Alfred.

We know little about that visit, but we do know that travel to the park was quite a challenge, even for the very wealthy. At best, the trip took two days. First, you boarded your private mahogany and velvet appointed railroad

Carriage crossing the bridge into camp. Mrs. Vanderbilt did not permit cars in the guest complex. *Photo from "Three Miles to Sagamore," a Vanderbilt family photo album from the 1940s donated to Sagamore by Alfred G. Vanderbilt. Photographer: Bert Clark Thayer.*

car at Cornelius Vanderbilt's Grand Central Station for a good night's sleep while traveling. The overnight trip ended either at North Creek, made famous by Teddy Roosevelt's inaugural ride after McKinley's assassination in 1901, or in Thendara. From either destination, you boarded a stagecoach to reach your steamer in order to cruise through the waterways via the Eckford or Fulton chains of lakes (Alfred Vanderbilt was actually an officer for the steamboat line on the Fulton chain). Those sojourners who disembarked at North Creek would take a stagecoach to the spacious Prospect House at Blue Mountain Lake, where the rooms were appointed with Edison light bulbs. At South Bay Inlet, you climbed into your carriage for the last few miles behind a horse. As you approached Sagamore, you were offered tantalizing glimpses of the magnificent Main Lodge through the trees. Your arrival was greeted with the flash of Roman candles as you crossed the guest bridge and alighted into the warm aura of camp, with its comforts of home.

Other Gilded Age families weathered similar obstacles to summer at Raquette Lake, where they were Margaret's Adirondack Park neighbors. J.P. Morgan was two miles away at Camp Uncas. Collis P. Huntington, the partner of railroad magnates Leland Stanford, Mark Hopkins and Charles Crocker, had a camp on Raquette Lake, as did Andrew Carnegie. With its ninety-nine miles of natural shoreline, its rousing public relations program fueled by W.W. Durant, the shortest standard-gauge railroad in the world at the Marion River Carry (a three-quarter-mile portage) and with its abundant recruited labor, Raquette Lake was the perfect place for July and August camping.

But for people like the Vanderbilts, Morgans and Carnegies, a two-day journey was too time consuming, so as railroad men, they bent all efforts to drive the railhead into Raquette Lake to complete the journey in a day. The town actually relocated to the new railhead and, in the process, changed its name from Durant to Raquette, which is French for snowshoe.

Contemporary visitors to Sagamore frequently comment on the remoteness of our camp and the long slow drive, four miles by gravel road, from the highway. For these Gilded Agers, though, privacy was the point and a remote location was the rule. Considering the fact that those who summered in the Adirondacks also had the option of homes in Newport, Palm Beach and Europe, we must acknowledge the lure of these mountain camps. Whether we believe that people like Alfred and Margaret liked being in nature in the sense that we know it today; or that they viewed nature as a challenge to be conquered, more in tune with their own time; or that the idea of using wilderness as recreation for the first time in history was enticing, we

The lean-to with balsam boughs spread as bedding. *Photo from "Three Miles to Sagamore," a Vanderbilt family photo album from the 1940s donated to Sagamore by Alfred G. Vanderbilt. Photographer: Bert Clark Thayer.*

recognize that the trip required commitment. After their strenuous journey, their stay was often for six weeks. In the early years, the Vanderbilts came for the last two weeks of July and the month of August.

Once here and settled in, these wealthy communities were out of the public eye. At Newport, Margaret's dinner gown, fare and guests would have been reported daily. At her Adirondack camp, her life was private, protected by Sagamore's remoteness and inaccessibility.

Besides the opportunity to escape scrutiny, campers believed that they were choosing a healthier environment. As Americans moved from farms to the cities, creating densely populated urban areas often lacking adequate infrastructure, the notion that wilderness life equaled healthy life gained currency, further encouraging Adirondack exploration. Alfred Vanderbilt's older brother died at Yale of typhoid. Queen Victoria's consort Prince Albert died when the sewers of London backed up. People were beginning to realize that in the city, summer heat and deadly fevers went hand in hand. The expression "escaping the heat of the city" did not merely indicate weather; it insinuated dire health threats as well. If you were in Margaret's place in the upper echelons of society, you did not spend the summer in the city waiting for a fever to waft you away: you left.

Mrs. Astor might have said to Mrs. Vanderbilt in polite conversation, "Tell me, my dear, when are you vacating to your Adirondack camp this year?" The reply from Mrs. Vanderbilt might have been, "We plan to vacate by July 10th." This term, "vacating," evacuating, gave us the concept of "vacations," which led to the American concept of "taking vacation," which supplanted the British concept and terminology of "taking holidays."

The vacation was invented in the Adirondacks.

The Architectural Legacy
of William West Durant

The Great Camps of the Adirondacks offered to their very comfortable owners an illusion of "roughing it," and Sagamore was no exception.

The grandest accomplishment of Adirondack developer William West Durant, the Sagamore that Margaret inherited featured a three-story Main Lodge, hot and cold running water, state-of-the-art sewer and septic systems and indoor plumbing. Plush and elegant in the style of the best European country estates where guests would hunt deer and shoot, it had nothing to do with our current version of camping.

Durant's father, Thomas Clark Durant, was a graduate of Albany Medical School. Not a doctor for long, he became general manager of the Union Pacific Railroad. He had been responsible for moving the Transcontinental Railroad west through the plains and on to Promontory Point. Looking at a picture of the Golden Spike ceremony reveals Dr. Durant in a long frock coat, tall and hunched. Known by all as a scoundrel, he established Credit Mobilier and created a scandal that involved members of Congress while he was building the Transcontinental.

Hurt economically in the panic of 1873, Durant Sr. then speculated that the Adirondacks were ripe for purchase. He bought vast tracts for three to six cents an acre to lock up the railroad rights and continued to buy until he owned almost one million acres. To develop this land, he enlisted the help of his son William West Durant. The younger Durant had to return from Europe, where his mother had reared him and his sister. Mrs. Durant had gone there to escape the tyranny of her husband.

William West arrived at Raquette Lake with his canoe. He set up camp on a beautiful point and started building Pine Knot, a project that would take him over a decade. Perhaps Pine Knot was named for a knot in a white pine tree, but another theory recalls the Victorian enjoyment of word play. Pine not, as in "pine not for me when I am gone," also means "don't yearn—you are at your own paradise, your Adirondack camp."

Durant's long tenure at Pine Knot was not merely to erect a complex of buildings. It was also to recruit labor that could learn to live in an unsettled, harsh wilderness and to put into place the infrastructure necessary to make land development possible. To get to a Great Camp, a road was needed. To get to the road, a steamship line was needed. To get to the steamship, a railroad was needed. To build a Great Camp, a crew of two hundred was needed. To recruit a crew of two hundred, food, housing, supplies, equipment, churches and schools for families were needed. Durant developed the transportation systems and provided the creature comforts necessary to accommodate his workers.

In 1895, he sold Pine Knot to Collis P. Huntington, one of the famous Big Four (Collis Huntington, Leland Stanford, Charles Crocker and Mark Hopkins) responsible for building the western portion of the Transcontinental Railroad. Collis P. Huntington was in business with the elder Durant. When William wanted to move on to his next project, he found it easy to ask Huntington to take Pine Knot off his hands for a fair price. Huntington enjoyed Pine Knot for only a short time; he died there in August 1895, and it remained empty for decades until it was given to the State University of New York at Cortland in 1947 to be used as an outdoor education center. Still in use for students, it is called Huntington to honor its former owner.

Durant's next project was Uncas. Built from 1893 to 1895 on Mohegan Lake, Uncas was designed with total separation of guest and service functions and with careful consideration of how the structures fit into the landscape. Durant visited the site in winter to see the land contours more easily so he could plan for building placements. Uncas manifests his clearest vision of the perfect great camp. The architecture was distinct in each portion of camp, with red board-and-batten structures for service and log or bark-covered buildings for guests. As at Pine Knot, there was a farm site to produce some of the workers' winter food, for building projects continued throughout the seasons. Uncas had a carriage house, barn, pig enclosure, workers' house, storage shed, pole barn and blacksmith shop, green house, pump house, root cellar and caretaker's cottage, in addition

Seven men in front of the barn, 1910s. *The Sagamore collection, courtesy of S. Roffe.*

to the bark-clad main house, dining hall complex, two cottages, icehouse, lean-to and boathouse. In one case at Uncas, location rather than strict function determined the architecture of the building. The caretaker's cottage is bark-covered instead of the more appropriate board-and-batten because it is visible from the dining hall complex and on the road to the main house. For many years, it housed the Callahan family, caretakers at Uncas. John and Mary Callahan both died in the cottage, and their granddaughter Mary was born there. Years later, Mary Callahan Patrick served, with her husband, as caretaker at Sagamore.

Durant had the poor judgment to use the beautiful camp as collateral for a loan with J.P. Morgan. When J.P. Morgan took it from him, he sold his yacht to acquire the funds needed to move on and began building his most magnificent camp, Sagamore. It must have been a bitter pill to swallow for Durant to lose Uncas, but he ordered his crew to push the road on for two miles to Shedd Lake (now Sagamore Lake) in order to begin again.

The crew started building in 1895, and in 1897 Durant moved into the grand Main Lodge. A three-story marvel of standard frame covered with

Carriage in front of the main lodge. *Photo from "Three Miles to Sagamore," a Vanderbilt family photo album from the 1940s donated to Sagamore by Alfred G. Vanderbilt. Photographer: Bert Clark Thayer.*

half-logs, it was the very model of a Swiss chalet. The full estate was 1,526 acres, and Durant situated his lodge, as at Uncas, on his favorite vantage point—overlooking the lake. He stocked both the lake and the land to ensure hunting and fishing success for visitors to Sagamore, the so-called sports who would come from the city to prove their woodland skills. He installed gaslights fueled by state-of-the-art compression chambers and pumps for the gasoline. He insisted on hot and cold running water and indoor plumbing for greater comfort than J.P. Morgan could enjoy at Uncas. He treated waste with a sewer and septic system that was better than those of many small towns. It was earlier, too, since it was installed before many smaller cities could claim one. He spent $250,000.

Around the turn of the century, three events brought him to his knees. The first was the death of Huntington who had served as his backer after his own father had died. The second was his divorce. The third was the lawsuit brought by his sister for the mismanagement of the family fortune. Ella probably needed to do only simple calculations to ascertain that by building camps Pine Knot, Uncas and Sagamore, William was spending far more than his third of the inheritance. T.C. Durant's will had left his fortune equally to his son, daughter and widow. William lost this suit, and he was denied further access to the remaining money, which was divided between his mother and sister.

At this point, Durant's entrepreneurial sense was tested. His years of development, marketing and selling were called into play. It is not hard to imagine his seeking out Alfred Vanderbilt, the fourth-generation Vanderbilt and the wealthiest young man in America, at a ball or theatrical opening and inviting him to Sagamore. Once seen, he suggested that Vanderbilt should buy Sagamore to use as a honeymoon cottage for his 1901 marriage. The deal was struck for $162,500.

Durant took the money to Blue Mountain Lake, where he began and abandoned the project of Camp Eagle's Nest, pioneering the concept of lakefront lots and a full golf course for second home owners. Defeated, he moved to Newcomb, where he became a hotel clerk and reportedly registered men who used to work for him. Eventually, he remarried and moved to North Creek. Our last photo of Durant is as an elderly gentleman sitting on a log bench at Uncas, broadly smiling. He died in 1934.

The Wealthiest Young Man in America

Alfred Gwynne Vanderbilt purchased Sagamore in 1901, and it remained in the Vanderbilt family until 1954. Margaret was not Sagamore's first Vanderbilt wife. That distinction belonged to Elsie French, who married Alfred and bore him a son, William H., before obtaining a divorce in 1908, allegedly for catching Alfred in a dalliance. Elsie took William to Newport, where he grew up and eventually distinguished himself, becoming governor of Rhode Island in 1939.

Alfred Gwynne was born on October 20, 1877, the same year that his great-grandfather Cornelius died. Dubbed "the Commodore," Cornelius made the Vanderbilt name and family fortune. Born in 1794, he borrowed $100 from his mother when he was sixteen in order to purchase a sailboat. From that humble beginning, he started a successful ferry service to Manhattan from his home on Staten Island. At the proper time in history, he converted his sailing fleet to steam engines. During the Gold Rush, he saw an opportunity to create a new route to California through Nicaragua. This lucrative but legally contested venture brought out his fiercely competitive nature and occasioned him to say to his former partners, when they tried to take over during the only vacation he had ever taken, "I will not sue you, for the law is too slow. I will ruin you." He then proceeded to do so.

During the Civil War, Lincoln called him to the White House to ask for his help. He joined the North's Civil War effort by providing the ship that disabled the *Monitor*'s effectiveness by bottling it up in the Elizabeth River in Virginia. After two weeks, he put the ship in the care of the navy; when he went

Alfred Gwynne Vanderbilt.

to reclaim it, he was told that it belonged to the U.S. government. After some legal wrangling, he was recommended for the Congressional Medal of Honor.

He was about seventy when he left shipping to enter railroading. Already a multimillionaire, Cornelius Vanderbilt expanded his fortune tenfold to $100 million.

His nemesis was Jay Gould, a railroad tycoon whose financial dealings led to Black Friday, one of the major scandals of the Ulysses Grant administration. In their battle for control of the New York Central, Vanderbilt and Gould both printed stock certificates in their basements at night to sell to each other the next morning. Vanderbilt famously said of Gould, "Never get into a pissing contest with a skunk." Vanderbilt's victory over Gould allowed him to build Grand Central Station, the boarding point for New Yorkers traveling to the Adirondacks. Despite these machinations, the Commodore should not technically be called a robber baron, as he predated them by a generation. Only one other antagonist among the railway investors, Daniel Drew, who later founded Wall Street, acted on Vanderbilt's grand scale.

So extensive was the Vanderbilt fortune that it was said that the Commodore had $100 million, the U.S. Treasury had $100 million and everyone else put together had $100 million That was the extent of the wealth of the privileged few during the Gilded Age.

As did most of the very wealthiest Americans, Vanderbilt emulated the practice of European aristocracy, leaving his fortune to his eldest son, William, who surprised the family by making even more money. William's two eldest sons, Cornelius and William, inherited the bulk of this fortune. Cornelius, grandson of the Commodore, was Alfred's father.

The third son of his family, Alfred Gwynne was not groomed to be the head of the family. His eldest brother, William, had that natural distinction. But William died tragically of typhoid while still a student at Yale. Cornelius, the second son, fell in love with William's fiancée and was disinherited on the day he married her. Alfred's younger brother, Reggie, who would become the father of Gloria Vanderbilt, famous for her designer jeans, was never considered well suited to lead the family.

Visitors get ready for a game of crack the whip out on the lake. Alfred's dog, Stormy, can be seen in the lower left corner.

Thus, when his father died in 1899, Alfred became head of house and the wealthiest young man in America, inheriting the bulk of the $80 million fortune. Traditionally in such families, the daughters and remaining sons would be given trust funds by the fortunate head of house. But Alfred did not stick to this protocol. Rather, he returned funds to his disinherited brother, and he also shared some of his fortune with his sisters.

Alfred was a sporting gentleman who enjoyed racing coach-and-four. His coach was in fact pulled by four white horses. At the turn of the century, he held the world land speed record for coaching races in England. He enjoyed many other sports and games and learned to drive an automobile but never learned to swim.

When he and Margaret decided to marry, it was undoubtedly recognized as a fitting, if gossip-provoking, match. They both loved the out-of-doors, horses and traveling, and they both knew the ins and outs of high society, where their divorces and the rumors of their marriage had been grist for the scandal mill. The wedding of Mrs. McKim and Mr. Vanderbilt was of course front-page news in the *Times*, but Newport high society claimed not to be surprised. They were married very quietly in Reigate, England, on a Sunday morning in December 1911 with only two witnesses present. Margaret wore a black silk traveling suit and black picture hat. She cabled her father, who had previously pledged to settle his entire fortune on her, after the ceremony. As newlyweds, she and Alfred traveled in England and France, where they raced and exhibited horses, went yachting and entertained. They lived in the newly constructed Vanderbilt Hotel, of which Alfred was the sole investor and owner, when they were in New York City. Their marriage produced two children: Alfred Gwynne Jr., born in 1912, followed in 1914 by their second son, George Washington Vanderbilt. The children were reared mostly in Lenox, Massachusetts, and away from Baltimore.

With their children, Margaret and Alfred spent joyful summers at Sagamore during their marriage, and the camp developed accordingly. While few buildings were erected during Alfred's marriage to Elsie, immediate expansion marked the earliest days of Margaret's tenure: an addition to Wigwam, and by 1914, a hydroelectric plant, tennis court and the famous bowling alley. To keep the camp on the cutting edge of technology, the powerhouse was positioned on the outlet from Sagamore Lake to Raquette Lake at the cascades where the falling water was harnessed for hydroelectricity. The power lines were buried underground to preserve the ambiance of camp. By 1915, a new laundry was opened with upstairs rooms for the British servants who always traveled with Mrs. Vanderbilt to serve at table.

But everything changed on May 4, 1915, when tragedy struck. A torpedo sank the *Lusitania*. Alfred was a passenger, returning to Europe to attend business meetings of the coaching society. As Margaret, with her young children, anxiously followed the dreadful news, word came that Alfred had died a hero, giving his life belt to a woman with a child who lived to report what he had done. The last words he was recorded as saying were to his valet, Ronald Denyer: "Come and let us save the kiddies." With that, he began loading children into lifeboats. His words, according to the *New York Times*, inspired a sermon by the bishop of London presiding at a meeting of the Waifs and Strays Society. It is sadly ironic that this young man, famed for accomplishment in a number of games and sports, could not swim—a skill that might have saved his life.

Expanding the Camp

Housing the Children

At Alfred's death, Sagamore was directly willed to Margaret. Given its remote location, the challenges of upkeep and the weight of her memories of the happier times with Alfred, it is probably true that many members of her social set cautioned her to sell Sagamore. But with a divorce and widowhood steeling her, she was prepared to become the chief steward of the camp. Her only overt act of sorrow after Alfred died was to order the removal of the foundation of the riding stable he had begun.

Margaret loved Sagamore and continued to travel to it every summer with her children and, in the course of time, her grandchildren, for the next thirty-nine years. In those years, she became known as the superb hostess of the "gaming crowd." Gaming referred to all sports and games, not just gambling as the word connotes today, and Sagamore was acclaimed its center.

Margaret married her third husband in 1918. Raymond T. Baker was head of the U.S. Mint. Their daughter, Gloria Marie, called Mimi, was born in 1920. Mimi was named debutante of the decade at her coming out in 1937.

Life for Margaret's children at Sagamore began on the third floor of the Main Lodge, where there was a large playroom and two adjoining rooms for sleeping and housing a nurse or nanny. There were, of course, a number of toys, including rocking horses for Mimi. There was also a round table built just a few inches from the floor that was a perfect fit for toddlers.

Margaret's three children: Alfred, Gloria and George.

As the children grew, they were moved to their own rooms at Lakeside Cottage, referred to as "the Incubator." Among the first additions to the Durant camp, the Incubator was an optimistic reflection of the expectations of Alfred and Elsie French for a large family, before their marriage ended in divorce. The Incubator is also where George and Alfred had their quarters as young men before their cottages were ready and eventually where the grandchildren spent their summers. It was directly on the lake and had its own dock. The grandchildren delighted in a rubber raft there. This cottage was set behind the bowling alley, and the grandchildren report that they considered it an adventure to walk through the trees on the path to the dining hall for meals. While the Incubator remains in service as housing for Sagamore caretakers, the lean-to where the grandchildren had sleep-outs is gone.

As the children came of age, cottages were built for each of them so that each could have a private bedroom, bath and sitting room. These cottages bear the names of Margaret's children: Alfred, George and Gloria. George's

Mr. and Mrs. George Vanderbilt in a guide boat. *Photo from "Three Miles to Sagamore," a Vanderbilt family photo album from the 1940s donated to Sagamore by Alfred G. Vanderbilt. Photographer: Bert Clark Thayer.*

Old laundry building converted to George's Cottage, 1930s. *The Sagamore collection, courtesy of G. Baltz.*

cottage was originally the laundry, converted into a bedroom and sitting room for him. The floor plans for Alfred (the same Alfred who later became the famous horseman who raced at Saratoga every year and who bred and owned Native Dancer) and Gloria's cottages are identical. Margaret's children enjoyed other buildings besides their cottages. In later years, George had an additional cottage built across the lake, which was accessed by canoe. His first wife said this was built so that she could cook for George because she was not permitted to use the Sagamore kitchen. Alfred and Mimi had their own lean-tos across the lake. George was also fond of spending time at Uncas, which his mother also owned from about 1948 until 1954.

IMPROVING THE INFRASTRUCTURE

From 1911 until Alfred's death in 1915, the Vanderbilts invested in upgrading Sagamore's systems. The pump house was built when they installed a new system to carry the pristine lake water through the existing cast-iron lines to all buildings. The pump house was especially important because its power

42

was needed to carry wastewater uphill to the leach fields in the workers' complex.

Prior to this installation, the camp had depended on a 100,000-gallon gravity system fed by springhouses. The reservoir and springhouses, now dilapidated, still exist on state land. It is interesting to note that the gravity-fed system at Uncas is still in limited service.

Margaret inherited the gasoline lighting system that had been installed by Durant when he built the camp. Professor Don Linebaugh explained to us that it was an invention of a Springfield, Massachusetts gas company and was designed for country estates. It consisted of a gasoline tank buried a required eighty feet away from the nearest building, pipes for circulating air over the gasoline in the tank in the ground and a compressor and mixer in the basement of the building. The gasoline fumes piped into the buildings were mixed as 15 percent gasoline vapors and 85 percent air. This mix was enough to provide light but was not highly flammable if treated with respect. Lighting the gasoline lights in camp was a responsibility of staff, not guests. Both the Main Lodge and Playhouse had these gasoline light systems, but they were soon replaced.

A piece of machinery in the power house.

The grandest achievement of this period was the powerhouse. From 1897 to 1913, Sagamore had gasoline lights, but Thomas Edison was changing that. Edison visited the Adirondacks and personally oversaw the installation of an electric bulb in every room of the Prospect House, a grand hotel at neighboring Blue Mountain Lake. The Vanderbilts harnessed their outlet to produce hydroelectricity and brought light bulbs to the Main Lodge and Wigwam, the guest house built primarily to meet the needs of young male guests, called "sports," who were frequent visitors to Sagamore. The wires were run up the gas conduits, and wall sconces held one gaslight and one electric bulb. The service building or new laundry, as well as the Chalet in the workers' complex, also called the Men's Camp, both plastered for strength and fire protection, were built with electricity as original equipment.

Knowing the Victorian fascination with air flow through their wooden homes (Sagamore boasts both transoms and floor grates in many buildings, notably the Playhouse), as well as gas lights and, later, electric wires using the gas conduits, it is not much of a surprise that so many American towns burned to the ground. Margaret herself suffered a fire at Holmwood, her beloved house in Lenox, Massachusetts. Sagamore considers itself fortunate to have had only one structure lost to fire. It was the cottage of Mr. Ryan, the electrician, which stood next to the barn.

SERVING THE GUESTS

Nothing was more important at Sagamore than the comfort and convenience of Margaret's guests. By 1915, Margaret realized that the laundry no longer accommodated the copious quantity of washing and ironing required at a camp where family and guests staying up to six weeks added their formal and informal clothing to the piles of daily linens from bedrooms, the kitchen and the dining hall. A much larger service building was completed that year with ample room for the new steam irons, heavy ironing boards and drying racks. There was also a room for the seamstress to repair or fashion clothing and space allotted for shining shoes and boots.

Upstairs were eleven bedrooms. Seven were for the British servants traveling with Mrs. Vanderbilt, and four were in a separate wing for the Collins family. Richard Collins was the caretaker from 1901 to 1924; he and his wife, Margaret Callahan Collins, had five children, all raised at Sagamore. Of all the buildings at Sagamore, this building makes the most elaborate use of bark work—an element chosen to emphasize the rusticity of

The large laundry facility that serviced the growing numbers of guests.

many buildings in the guest complex—but its metal roof labels it a building for work, not for guests. On the first floor, next to the laundry room, was a sitting room with a brick fireplace for the Collins family. The size of the service building, in conjunction with the size of the dining hall, are the two most obvious examples of the kind of support system in the guest complex needed to care for the huge numbers of visitors entertained at Sagamore. In 1924, the year the Collins family bought the Hedges at Blue Mountain Lake and moved from Sagamore, Margaret ordered a formidable expansion of the dining facilities to accommodate her ever-expanding guest list.

The only Sagamore workers who made personal contact with the guests were the guides; because they fraternized with guests, they had a special place in the hierarchy of the camp. Locals who knew the woods, they prided themselves not only on hunting and fishing but also on storytelling. Guides were well versed in the wilderness skills necessary for keeping the "sports" warm, dry, well fed, out of danger and entertained. Their housing was a narrow room behind the dining hall and the staff lounge where they ate with other workers. The lean-to beside the staff galley was for cleaning fish and game. Guides could walk through the staff area directly into the back entrance of the kitchen where the chef would take charge of the catch. There are also five bedrooms over the kitchen where various staff members lived.

The icehouse was attached to the dining hall. This part of camp is architecturally complex. The covered walkway joined the icehouse, staff quarters and original laundry to the dining hall. Looking at the rooflines from the neighboring service building, the dining hall complex reminds one of the rooftops of London. It is a nightmare of maintenance. A fence separated the entire service area in the lower complex from the eyes of the Vanderbilt guests.

Margaret always realized that fine dining would be central to a pleasant stay at Sagamore, and she planned accordingly. Durant's 1897 dining hall consisted only of a porch and a hall with a fireplace, which seated just twelve or fifteen at a large, log-based table. A chandelier that had been forged in the Sagamore blacksmith shop hung overhead covered by a Victorian cloth shade. In 1901, the Vanderbilts walked into the hall and realized that it would be too small for their grander style of entertaining. They ordered the workers to take Durant's plan for the original dining hall and flop it over as a mirror image to double the space. The addition had a matching corner fireplace, a matching chandelier and a matching table, built by different artisans to identical specifications. The ceiling was decorated with faux beams, and hunting trophies hung on the paneled walls. The large tables were placed end-to-end between the fireplaces.

This space was sufficient until 1924, when the story tells us that Margaret took a stick in one hand and her caretaker in the other, walked outside the dining hall and sketched the plan for a huge expansion into the dirt. She turned to her caretaker and told him she had invited sixty-five people for Christmas dinner and that she expected the addition to be ready. His reply could only have been, "Yes, ma'am." The expansion more than doubled the size of the hall. It included a bay window large enough for seating for twelve at its distinctive circular table. Her architectural instincts were sound; the dining hall is breathtaking.

Breakfast did not always require use of the dining hall because trays could be taken to each guest's room. It was hearty fare with creamed chicken over biscuits, a Sagamore favorite. There was also the option of a traditional,

The Vanderbilts' Adirondack Retreat

Dining hall interior, 1930s. *The Sagamore collection, courtesy of G. Baltz.*

Beautiful china that graced the tables of Sagamore. *Photograph by D. Scranton.*

hearty English breakfast. Lunches could be an outdoor picnic in the lean-tos or on the grounds (an elaborate entertainment with tablecloths, china and servants), but the dining hall was used to its full potential for Margaret's elegant dinners.

Dinners at Margaret's Sagamore were formal. Guests dressed for cocktails at the Main Lodge and then entered the hall from the back, where they were seated at the round table or the log-based tables that had been moved from the original expansion of the Durant dining hall. These twin tables are considered too wide by our modern standards because they are difficult to speak across. In Gilded Age terms, however, they were perfect because gentlemen had dinner partners; each addressed the lady on his left during the first course, the lady on his right during the second course and then alternated throughout the courses until the meal was over and the men withdrew for port and cigars.

Service was provided by British liveried servants who always traveled with Margaret to serve at table. A chef from Delmonico's was often invited to prepare meals, and formal dinner menus were written in French on cards preprinted with Sagamore scenes. "Sagamore" was engraved on the handles of the silver plated flatware. The dinnerware, manufactured by Higgens and Seiter, was designed exclusively for Sagamore with a pattern of spruce trees circling the gold-trimmed rim. Margaret is said to have challenged her guests to discover which of them had the plate with the raccoon hiding in the tree. This was merely an example of her playfulness because there was, of course, no raccoon. Crystal-stemmed glasses carrying the hand-painted tree and gold motif in at least four shapes for wines, champagne and aperitif also graced the table. There were dozens of individual serving pieces. In the Sagamore collection, for instance, are examples of hot chocolate pots with golden handles.

The menu was quite varied. Fish and game were among those things served as guests brought in the deer, birds and fish that they hunted or caught with the help of their Adirondack guides. This fare was elegantly prepared and then served to the awaiting guests from silver platters carried ceremoniously by the British servants. One menu included turtle soup, mushrooms on toast points, trout, salad, venison, sorbet and strawberries with clotted cream. Later in her tenure as Sagamore's hostess, after she had been to Hawaii, Margaret enjoyed pineapple in many dishes. A surprising dietary addition was noted in early accounts of Sagamore meals: coffee gelatin. This gelatin recipe was probably eaten by guests and perhaps sampled by workers. Jell-O was invented in 1897, the year Sagamore was first occupied.

Workers and artisans ate in the upper complex (also called the caretaker's village), where the wives of the division heads or hired cooks prepared foods that we know as regular fare of farmers and lumberjacks, such as biscuits, flapjacks, maple syrup, venison and pie for breakfast and dinner. Workers made up to one hundred gallons of maple syrup each year for the Vanderbilts to use and give to friends. This was an enormous job in the late winter and early spring. Trees were tapped and sap collected in buckets that were carried to the sugar shack near the farm site, where fifty gallons of sap boiled down over wood fires to one gallon of syrup. The Adirondack recipes using maple syrup were not quaint but practical because sugar was in short supply. Meat and potatoes would have been the rule for the workers, although their diet could be enriched by the delicate lettuces and salad vegetables grown—primarily for the

The camp's employees and their families lived on the grounds in their own little village, which even had a schoolhouse for the children.

The greenhouse and upper garden. *Photo from "Three Miles to Sagamore," a Vanderbilt family photo album from the 1940s donated to Sagamore by Alfred G. Vanderbilt. Photographer: Bert Clark Thayer.*

guests—in the camp garden in the summertime and by the produce of the farm meadow.

There was a two-level greenhouse at the top of the garden where plants were started so that, in spite of the long Adirondack winters, they could be ripened by mid-July when the family arrived. They might have been grown

Like much of the Adirondack Park, Great Camp Sagamore blooms in the spring and the summer. The camp used a greenhouse and many gardens to maintain its flora.

Ice cutting on Sagamore Lake, 1930s. *The Sagamore collection, courtesy of G. Baltz.*

in the upper portion of the garden, where the parking lot is now situated, or on the terraces by the bowling alley. There was a formal portion of the garden with a central "knot" and four quadrants of a large square bed. The paths through and around the garden are overgrown but still visible. The flower garden was protected by a large fence that ostensibly kept the deer out. Flowers for the rooms were gathered from this garden at Margaret's request.

Although the garden might have produced the root vegetables, potatoes, onions, carrots and cabbages that the workers stored in the root cellar for winter use, it is more likely that these were grown at the farm site across the lake. Milk and dairy products for everyone in camp were provided year-round by cows that spent summers at the farm site and winters in the barn with the horses. The workers' complex building that we call the Hen House, across from the barn, served as a gigantic chicken coop. Its yard was fenced in to protect the poultry from foxes and other predators. A large population of fowl was very practical because workers could use the meat or the eggs. Poultry also reproduced quickly.

Cool drinks in summer were possible in either part of camp because each had its own icehouse. Ice was stored in wood chips and sawdust after it was harvested from the lake in the dead of winter. Like all of nature's bounty, ice had both good and bad years, and the ice harvest was the most dangerous job in camp. The head caretaker would have taken an auger daily to the lake to test the thickness of the ice and would have paid close attention to rising and falling temperatures that could cause the development of undesirable air pockets. Dense ice at sixteen to eighteen inches thick was the optimum for harvest. Blocks weighed about three hundred pounds each. No matter how difficult the harvest, ice was a necessary component of proper summer entertaining.

Sports and Games

M argaret once said that she loved all sports and games. An avid and proficient croquet player, she was posthumously inducted into the Croquet Hall of Fame at Newport. Her wickets still grace the lawn at Sagamore. Large and heavy in the British style, the wickets from Margaret's era required a bigger ball and a more sizable mallet (somewhere between the size of a current croquet mallet and a polo mallet) for the game. Margaret was called a "bloodthirsty" player, and it is not likely that anyone who accepted her challenge would win.

She shot skeet from the porch of the Main Lodge. A few years ago, a Sagamore intern donned his scuba gear and retrieved several of the old clay pigeons from the lake. Margaret was a deadeye shot, so we believe that the ones that were still whole must have belonged to her guests. Her sons, George and Alfred, often went on hunting and safari trips; Alfred actually hunted lions in Africa with Hemingway. The hunting trophies that decorate the walls at Sagamore are a collection from many parts of the world, not just the Adirondacks. At least one prize fish mounted in the dining hall at Sagamore belongs to Margaret.

Margaret continued to stock the lake and keep guides on staff so that her guests could go hunting and fishing. She also had beautiful Adirondack guide boats docked at the boathouse (one of Durant's original 1897 buildings) for the use of her guests. After a morning in the woods, it would have been a pleasure to take a guide boat out for the afternoon. The numbers of afternoon picnics and teas in the lean-tos are countless.

A nice catch of deer, 1927. *The Sagamore collection, courtesy of A. Shatraw.*

Guide boats at the boathouse on Sagamore Lake. *Photo from "Three Miles to Sagamore," a Vanderbilt family photo album from the 1940s donated to Sagamore by Alfred G. Vanderbilt. Photographer: Bert Clark Thayer.*

Bowling alley interior, 1930s. *The Sagamore collection, courtesy of G. Baltz.*

Tennis and bowling both became available at Sagamore in 1914 with the construction of the tennis court and bowling alley. Margaret used to invite young men from the Yale tennis team to play with her sons and the guests. The caretaker's children would set the pins in the semi-outdoor bowling alley built by Brunswick, Balke and Cullender. The lanes eventually fell into disrepair, and it was not until the early 1990s that they were put back into use. A call to Brunswick to help with the project brought back the reply that they no longer had anyone on staff who could refinish wooden lanes. Everyone now works on plastic and composite! So Sagamore recruited a guide boat builder, very familiar with wood, who directed the repair job. When he got down through the layers of dirt that had covered the original lanes and removed the old surfaces, the lanes were exactly where they had been placed in 1914, free of cracks, warps or damage because the workers who had installed the lanes lived at Sagamore year-round, year after year, and they understood Adirondack winters. The frost level at Raquette Lake is seventy-one and a half inches; the workers dug down six feet and then began pouring reinforced concrete. Brunswick installed the alleys on top of this firm foundation, and they have remained in place ever since. In winter, we simply pull down the canvas curtains, which protect the lanes from blowing snow. In spring, the curtains go up at the first opportunity so that the building can breathe. Water damage and the threat of fire are the two greatest threats to the wooden buildings of the Adirondacks.

The adjacent Playhouse was the site of evening activities. A player piano with many piano rolls stood at the ready, and Mr. Paige, Margaret's friend, was often called upon to play. There were card tables and jigsaw puzzles. A pool table eventually joined a ping-pong table, and in the corner stood the roulette wheel. Adirondack architect William Coulter built the Playhouse (and later went on to build Topridge for Margery Merriweather Post of Post cereals) as a copy of Durant's Main Lodge. It was both spacious enough for grand parties and far enough away from sleeping quarters to allow parties to last into the wee hours. The parties were well fueled; there was no Prohibition at Sagamore. Liquor flowed in from Canada. The bushel basket hanging in the barn is also an important artifact, showing that the workers, too, enjoyed their own games, including the newly invented basketball.

As Alfred, George and Gloria grew to adulthood, they expanded on Margaret's entertaining with their own. Her grandchildren report that one summer they stayed at Uncas because Sagamore was too full of spirited activity to accommodate them. We now believe that this was the postwar year that General George C. Marshall and Madame Chiang Kai-Chek visited Sagamore. Madame Chiang's entourage was so large that the grandchildren had to give up their rooms and move to Uncas.

The Playhouse was the site for many indoor sports and games, including puzzles, cards, ping-pong, pool and roulette.

Sagamore Pets and Animals

The most famous pet at Sagamore was Inky, a black cocker spaniel owned by Fiona "Fifi" Witchell, Margaret's best friend. Fifi was apparently something of a character. Workers reported that you had to be patient to see Fifi because her cigarette holder was so long that she entered a room a full minute after her cigarette got there. Margaret's own cigarette holders were from Tiffany. Fifi probably let Inky sleep on the foot of her bed and eat very tasty orts from the dining hall. He must have had the full run of camp and the carriage trails. Inky arrived for the last time at Sagamore in a box with a note asking that he be buried at his favorite place. Margaret depended on her caretaker, Mr. Callahan, to find the most appropriate burial spot. A place at the back of the garden was selected, and soon both black wreath and headstone arrived. Engraved on the headstone were the words, "Always the best friend I will ever have. FI," along with Inky's dates, August 1, 1920–October 16, 1936. Inky's August birthday still occasions a party by current staff.

Stormy was Alfred's dog. He is depicted in a shot in the dining hall sitting on Alfred's lap at the head of the table at a 1903 winter party.

The upper complex also held a deer pen. Part of the well-rusted wire fence still remains. The guests fed a fawn that was quite tame. Deer feeding extended into winter. The feed was broadcast on top of the ice, where the deer gathered at about 4:00 p.m. each day to eat. Deer also trim the cedars around the lake by standing on the ice and feeding on any of the lower branches they can reach. This clearly defined line around

Alfred Vanderbilt, dog Stormy and friends, 1902, in the dining hall. *The Sagamore collection, courtesy of Alfred Vanderbilt.*

the lake is so noticeable that visitors often ask Sagamore staff members about this "browse line."

The Vanderbilts always loved horses. Workhorses and carriage horses were housed in the barn. There was at least one pony in camp to pull Mimi's cart. Johnny Hoy was the head teamster entrusted with the care of the horses. He lived in the barn boss apartment over the stables with his wife and daughter. Horses and carriages were held in such high regard by Margaret that when roads finally came to Raquette Lake and Vanderbilt guests and friends began driving to Sagamore, she made the rule that cars could not drive into the guest complex. She did not want to ruin the ambiance of camp. At that point, the barn was enlarged to become part-garage to care for vehicles that were mandatorily parked there.

With horses and carriages such an important part of Margaret's and Alfred's lives, the accident that killed Johnny Hoy was a grim irony. The family's love of horses and Alfred's championships in coaching were facts. With Alfred's untimely death, Margaret carried on what would

Horses were always a part of life at Sagamore. *Photo from "Three Miles to Sagamore," a Vanderbilt family photo album from the 1940s donated to Sagamore by Alfred G. Vanderbilt. Photographer: Bert Clark Thayer.*

Above and below: Carriage wreck that killed John Hoy on the road near the farm site, August 1917. *The Sagamore collection, courtesy of H. Collins.*

have been their joint pleasure of teaching their young sons to love horses and riding. It was a frequent event for the boys to take carriage rides around Sagamore Lake on the broad carriage road. On this day in 1916, Johnny Hoy hitched a team to the carriage, loaded up the boys and their nanny and began the drive.

It was a beautiful, quiet, windless day that was suddenly broken by the sound of horses wildly racing back to camp dragging their traces. The buckles and leather straps jerking behind them made an audible clatter crossing the wooden bridge where workers and Margaret raced to intercept the frightened team. The team had broken loose from the carriage, and the fragmented pieces of the carriage still attached to the trappings threw the men into a frenzied foot race on the trail to find the scene of the freak accident.

It was dreadful. Johnny had been killed outright by a falling tree, and Alfred was severely wounded. He suffered a deep gash to his forehead, nearly scalping him, and his legs were broken above the knees where the tree had hit him as he sat next to Johnny on the front seat of the carriage. He carried a lifelong scar on his forehead.

Johnny's body was taken to North Creek for burial. Margaret gave her widow's weeds to Mrs. Hoy and let her remain at Sagamore with her daughter until other arrangements for her well-being could be made. The blacksmith forged an iron cross memorial that remains on the trail today to mark the site of the accident. To our knowledge, Johnny Hoy was the only person ever killed at Sagamore.

Living in the Workers' Village

Margaret's role as hostess required much more than deciding dinner menus. In 1915, when Alfred died, the young Margaret inherited the responsibility of overseeing several building projects that were under construction. The carpenter/paint shop, important for all the wood projects around camp, was completed along with the Chalet, or Men's Camp, for staff housing. In her sorrow, Margaret canceled the orders to build a riding stable, but in future years she would oversee the construction of cabins for her children, the expansion of the dining hall and a new pumping system for water service.

Workers and artisans were employed to execute all these projects, and one of her chief concerns would have been to provide the proper buildings, services and equipment to support the myriad activities of a year-round working camp. The workers' area of the camp was a village with workshops, barns, housing, storage and a schoolhouse for the workers' children.

Only men who had worked their way up the ladder had their wives and families in camp. Others would visit their families in Inlet, Blue Mountain Lake, Indian Lake or Old Forge during breaks. Meanwhile, they lived together in a chalet-style building so large that visitors today frequently ask if it is the Main Lodge. It has nine bedrooms upstairs and an open attic space that could have bunked thirty to forty men.

The addition under the shed roof was added for Tom and Millie Callahan, who had been caretakers at Uncas. Relatives of the Collins family, they were the first caretaking family to live in the Chalet when they moved from

Caretaker's complex in winter, 1930s. *The Sagamore collection, courtesy of G. Baltz.*

The Vanderbilts' Adirondack Retreat

These cabins housed employees of Sagamore and reflected the visible division between the rich and poor during the Gilded Age.

Workers in the farm complex. *Photo from "Three Miles to Sagamore," a Vanderbilt family photo album from the 1940s donated to Sagamore by Alfred G. Vanderbilt. Photographer: Bert Clark Thayer.*

Uncas to Sagamore in 1924. Their daughter, Mary Callahan Patrick, and son-in-law later assumed caretaking responsibilities. Margaret thought that Mary Callahan Patrick's five children needed more space than she could allot them in the service building, where the Collins family had lived, so she provided a sitting room in the front of the Chalet, in the space that now serves as a gift shop. A partition with a door divided the sitting room from the kitchen area where the family and many of the workers ate. Feeding and

Top: Collins children with fish, in front of kitchen extension, about 1913. *The Sagamore collection, courtesy of H. Collins.*

Bottom: Main Lodge—Collins children at winter sports, about 1915. *The Sagamore collection, courtesy of H. Collins.*

Opposite: Schoolhouse—Collins children and teacher. *Back, left to right*: Dick Collins (Richard Jr.), Patrick, teacher and John Collins. *Front, left to right*: Tom and Margaret, about 1914. *The Sagamore collection, courtesy of H. Collins.*

housing the workers was always one of Margaret's primary concerns; she would occasionally visit Mrs. Patrick in her sitting room to discuss upcoming projects with her.

Women in camp had the tasks of cooking for the crew, tending the chickens, canning and doing laundry and mending. In winter, the women would make Turkey red curtains with rings to slide onto rods and would sew matching skirts for radiators for the guest quarters. Red was Margaret's favorite color for Sagamore; because it faded so easily in the light, brown paper would be fitted to the windows after Margaret left for the season to try to preserve the color in the material.

Workers' children had their own schoolhouse. It was originally completed in 1911 as housing for the men, but the crew soon outgrew it and moved it in 1915 to a location next to the blacksmith shop. Children from caretaking families from Sagamore, Uncas and Kamp Kill Kare would all attend classes in the school. In the Sagamore collection is a photograph of the Collins children in front of the schoolhouse. High school was in Raquette Lake, and Margaret Collins Cunningham, youngest of the Collins family, reported that she never missed a day even in the deepest snows of winter. Workhorses would have been hitched to wooden plows or to snow rollers to flatten and harden the snow on the road to keep it passable for the important trip to school each day.

Bark and Artisans

CREATING THE RUSTIC STYLE

Arguably the most important legacy of the Great Camp era was its support of the skilled artisans who built the camps and perfected the Adirondack style. People who worked at Sagamore and the other camps often stayed for years. They were given room, board, about a dollar a day in salary and the support necessary to hone their skills. Perhaps the wealthy owners of the Great Camps have not received sufficient credit for the level of support they provided for these craftsmen. At the time, given the primitive state of efforts to settle the Adirondacks, such support would have seemed an obvious necessity. Nowadays, this near-communal existence, which provided time for perfection of various useful rustic crafts, is viewed as a positive byproduct of the Great Camps. Craftsmen and craftswomen lived in a closed community and worked daily with each other in an apprentice-to-master relationship. Winters were bustling with activity at Sagamore, for the long cold period was ideal for perfecting skills.

As he began his Adirondack projects, Margaret's predecessor, W.W. Durant, could not assume the presence of a workforce in the remote Adirondacks. Recruiting workers was a challenge. There are stories of foremen going to Ellis Island to watch the men and women disembarking. If they needed masons, they would look for men with trowels; if carpenters were needed, they kept an eye out for hammers and saws. They could offer transportation to the Adirondacks, room and board and a job. The best recruitment would have been among family members; it is no surprise that the Callahans followed the Collins family as the caretakers at Sagamore because they were joined by marriage.

Durant would have had master craftsmen, but he also would have had raw talent. A young man hired to split wood might have saved the best logs to build himself a bed. If it came out well, Durant would have known and gone for an inspection, whereupon he probably would have recruited the young man to make more or might have paired him with a master. There were several fine carpenters at Sagamore. Seraphin Lanteigne was a noted master carpenter; carpenters like Charlie Hunt also branched off into boat building and snowshoe and toboggan construction as required by need. Albert "Allie" Roblee was also known for furniture building.

These craftsmen often had more than one skill. Gardener George Wilson also created twig mosaic furniture. He was known for the intricate star pattern of closely matched twigs often used for tabletops. Men artistically adopted the natural materials available to them, and the rustic style was born.

One characteristic of "rustic" carpenter work is that the bark is often left on the wood. Durant's workers left the bark on many logs used to build and decorate his structures, but they also applied bark as sheathing to give the appearance of the rustic. If the tree were going to be used with the bark on, the men would have cut it in the deepest part of winter. Twenty below was good, but thirty below was better because the tree would have extracted every drop of sap and stored it well below the surface in its roots. The bark would tightly adhere to the tree.

For the bark siding that covers so many of the guest buildings at Sagamore, the tree was cut in early spring as the sap began to rise and the bark began to "slip." These trees were thrown into the lake and soaked before a tool called a spud was used to remove the bark from the full circumference of the tree in four-foot lengths. Think of a label on a soup can that is cut lengthwise and removed in one piece. The bark would have been scraped to rid it of any vestiges of sap. In both of these methods, winter cutting and spring cutting, the end product was material cleaned of food for insects. The remarkable staying power of Sagamore's bark makes one wonder why we ever bothered to invent aluminum siding. Here, the bark used comes from white cedar and white spruce. Perhaps Margaret did not like the look of birch bark that is used in other Great Camps.

Stones for the masons were quarried in the Adirondacks. Some fieldstone was also used. Our masonry is superb except in the case of the main fireplace in the dining hall. Its poor craftsmanship was undoubtedly because

George Wilson, an artisan at Sagamore, working outside.

of the speed required to finish the project on Margaret's schedule. There are twenty-six stone fireplaces in Sagamore's buildings, including one at the bowling alley added on as an afterthought. Perhaps bowling outdoors proved a bit chillier than expected. Schuyler Kathan was Sagamore's most well-known mason, responsible for many of the wonderful fireplaces, each

71

with a distinctive stone or log mantle piece. Construction of the wonderful fireplace in the lounge of the Wigwam, the building designed primarily for male guests, involved using stones that were set in place with the moss still on them. Workers had to spray the soft plant with water to keep it green. In the Main Lodge, the room originally used by Durant features a fireplace with a sunburst designed in reddish mortar. The three-tiered fireplace in the Playhouse is so weighty that it was warping the building until the drainage was rerouted around it. Because of their size, fireplaces were built first and the buildings put around them. In the lounge of the Main Lodge, the saddle notches cut from the stones where the beams are fitted in are clearly observable.

The beams in the Main Lodge are constructed of full-length spruce trunks. On the outside of the building, logs were added as finishing touches to make the building look like a log structure. It is not. Rather, it is standard frame with a half-log façade. Constructing buildings with these emblems of rusticity was not a simple endeavor. Allie Roblee is said to have been the builder most capable of calculating log shrinkage, a vital skill at the camps.

The panels on the walls inside the lodge are each shaped perfectly to fit the stone they abut, attesting to the kind of time and quality of craftsmanship employed at Sagamore. Although clear lumber was readily available from the sawmill at Utowana, Durant chose knotty wood instead because he liked the "rustic" feel. Knots dry out at a different rate than the rest of the panel and pop from the wood, so each knot had to be specially treated to ensure that it would stay in place. Leaving the knots in place actually created more work, not less, as one might assume.

The blacksmiths at Sagamore created remarkable decorative work. The doors at the Main Lodge and Playhouse are most noteworthy, with their heavy hinges and large locks requiring huge forged keys. The door at the Main Lodge is unabashedly that of a castle. Charles Dougherty and Jimmy Leffler are the blacksmiths credited with the chandeliers in the lodge and dining hall that marry copper and iron. Fireplace tools, screens and andirons for all the fireplaces in the guest complex were also forged. In the Playhouse, form was functional: the blacksmith-forged long bar light cast illumination on the pool table. Margaret ordered another fixture when she rearranged the room to hold a ping-pong table. Throughout the camp, the consummate craftsmanship inspired by the American arts-and-crafts movement makes Sagamore a standing monument to its artisans.

The traditional arts were a way of life, and responsibility for nurturing these arts fell largely to the head caretaker. Caretakers had plentiful skills of their own, along with the ability to manage. When Margaret left Sagamore at the end of August, the caretaker was responsible for all operations. We have early examples of letters from the owners of Sagamore to the caretaker discussing building projects, supplies and workers. And when the landlord wasn't there, who "owned" Sagamore? Surely the claim can be made that the people who lived year-round and raised their families at Sagamore were the real proprietors.

The Irish potato famine brought to America the immigrant families who would become Sagamore's head caretakers. The Collins family settled in North Creek, and the Callahans settled in Chestertown, where they became farmers. John Callahan, first Durant's, then J.P. Morgan's caretaker at Uncas, hired his brother-in-law, Richard Collins, to go to work at Sagamore. The family of Richard Collins helped Margaret's transition from wife to widow in charge of Sagamore. They were with Alfred from 1901 to his death in 1915 and remained with Margaret until 1924.

Margaret brought Tom and Millie Callahan from Uncas to be her next caretakers in 1924. After their daughter Mary became Mrs. Patrick, she and her husband—like Richard and Margaret Collins before them—bore and raised five children at Sagamore. They stayed only briefly after Syracuse University took over because Mr. Patrick didn't like the way the university cared for the camp. When the Patricks left, Bruce and Mary Darling of Syracuse moved into the Chalet and raised their family there. The building in the 1970s housed a youth conservation corps (YCC) program.

Sagamore's caretaker since 1985 has been Bob Heinsler. He lives with his family in Lakeside Cottage, formerly called the Incubator, and he is the first recipient of the Callahan-Collins Caretaking Award.

"Call Me Mrs. Emerson"

Alfred stated in his will that Margaret should inherit Sagamore, and that very rich aspect of her adult life is our major concern here. But she had a life outside Sagamore, of course. After Alfred's death, she bought Holmwood, a forty-seven-room mansion on a 316-acre estate in Lenox, Massachusetts. Her other large inherited property was Arcadia, Isaac Emerson's antebellum rice plantation in Georgetown, South Carolina. He had discovered and purchased it while cruising the coastline in his yacht. He also gave her Sagamore Farms in Maryland.

And there were other marriages, as well as other estates. Margaret had known Ray Baker since before her marriage to Alfred. After they were wed in 1918, they were often at Sagamore together. In 1928, she returned to Reno, where she had a residence, and divorced him. Mimi was eight years old, Alfred was sixteen and George was fourteen. Margaret and Charles Minot Amory, a member of Boston's high society, were married soon after, but the union lasted less than five years. They divorced in 1934. At this point, Margaret was fifty and declared that she was done with marriages. She legally reassumed her maiden name, and told her staff, "Call me Mrs. Emerson."

She devoted herself, according to her *Times* obituary, to her war charities, her children and raising horses, but her work with the Red Cross was vastly more significant than the simple allusion to war charities suggests. Margaret's truest claim to fame was her Red Cross work during World War II. Named head of their operations in the Pacific, she was devoted to

Margaret's bedroom at Sagamore.

recreational therapy for the injured and homesick soldiers. She often paid for transportation for shell-shocked and sick boys who couldn't afford to travel. For her humanitarian efforts she was awarded the highest civilian honors. And for her devotion to the care of others, she was reinstated into the Catholic Church.

From 1934, when her first granddaughter was born to George and his wife Lucille (née Parsons), until after World War II, Sagamore was the favorite summer place for Margaret to take her grandchildren. They called her "Tutu," Hawaiian for grandmother. George's daughter, Lulu, and Mimi's children, Sandra and Tony Topping, were annual visitors. Alfred's children were there less frequently, but all remember the lake, fishing, deer and the bowling alley. On the frame of a doorway in the Main Lodge are marks indicating measurements of the growth of Margaret's children and grandchildren.

But following World War II, attitudes toward great estates dramatically changed. They were recognized as holdovers from a bygone era and as monsters of maintenance. Faster travel took passengers to far-reaching corners of the earth more exotic than the Adirondacks. Margaret had grown fond of Hawaii and found it harder to convince her busy family and friends to visit her at Sagamore. The final argument in her decision to divest herself of Sagamore came from Mother Nature. A hurricane-force windstorm in 1950 devastated the beautiful surrounding forest, and Margaret could not bear to look at the destruction. Thinking she was protecting the Sagamore she loved, she gifted it to Syracuse University in 1954.

Just six years later, Margaret died of a heart attack at her New York City apartment at 1020 Fifth Avenue, two days into the new decade of the 1960s. A solemn requiem mass was held for her at Saint Patrick's Cathedral.

Sagamore After Margaret

Margaret could not have predicted the challenges that Sagamore would face after the years of her stewardship. She must have believed in 1954 when she deeded it to Syracuse University that it would both enjoy and care for her beloved camp. The reality was that Syracuse used the camp for twenty years while deferring necessary maintenance, and when the costs for repairs became too large, it divested itself of the property. It logged the land, auctioned the furnishings and hunted for a buyer.

In the mid-'70s, the only party interested in the large white elephant was the State of New York, and it was only interested because of the 1,526 acres of land that, when purchased, would be added to the "forever wild" park holdings, as defined in Article 14 of the New York State Constitution, which says that land owned by the state in the Adirondack or Catskill Parks must remain forever wild. If there are man-made improvements on such land, the improvements must be removed or allowed to fall back into the earth. Syracuse University and the state agreed that Sagamore would be permitted to fall down.

At the eleventh hour, the Preservation League of New York and the Department of Environmental Conservation officials were persuaded that a nonprofit organization should be allowed to bid at auction on the bark-covered buildings. The red buildings of the workers' complex were judged too unimportant to save. A 7.7-acre parcel where the guest complex is located was removed from the state's deed, and a nonprofit organization, the Adirondack Humanistic Education Center, headed by Barbara Glaser and

Above: Ninth Sagamore Army Materials Research Conference, 1962, "Fundamentals of Deformation Processing." Photograph taken in front of the Main Lodge. *The Sagamore collection, courtesy of Syracuse University.*

Below: Syracuse University visitors dine in the dining hall at Great Camp Sagamore in the years after Margaret's death.

In the late twentieth century, Syracuse University visitors still enjoyed one of Margaret's favorite activities, playing croquet, on the grounds.

Howie Kirschenbaum, won the bid. It moved in, changed the name of the nonprofit organization to the National Humanistic Education Center, and later to Sagamore Institute, and began using Sagamore as an educational conference center.

Within a decade, Glaser and Kirschenbaum realized that the guest complex needed to be reunited with the workers' complex, and they began a "Save Sagamore" movement. Because parkland is protected, the people of the state had to vote on a referendum to allow Sagamore Institute to buy back its own red workers' complex buildings. On a triumphant day in 1983, the voters said "yes," and Sagamore Institute purchased a piece of land to trade into the forest preserve while the ten acres of the workers' complex were traded out. Sagamore was reunited and placed under a forty-two-page covenant aimed at preservation.

In 1989, the board approved language proposed by new directors Beverly Bridger and Michael Wilson that rededicated Sagamore's programs to an environmental mission well suited to the camp. Sagamore was reincorporated under the Department of Education as a cultural institute named Sagamore Institute of the Adirondacks. The board of trustees, staff and donors are dedicated to the stewardship of Great Camp Sagamore and to its use for educational and interpretive purposes.

Maintaining and Preserving Sagamore

A rule of thumb in preservation is that fewer owners result in better care of a facility. Sagamore has had only four owners—William West Durant, the Vanderbilt family, Syracuse University and its current not-for-profit owner, Sagamore Institute of the Adirondacks—which should indicate a decent record of care. However, Syracuse University owned Sagamore for twenty years and practiced "deferred maintenance" as its policy. You can imagine use by college students for one year, much less twenty, without maintenance.

A second rule is that poverty can be a good preservation partner. Think of this—poor owners do not have the money to make changes to property. They are not likely to tear down a wall and build a new wing, nor are they likely to install a swimming pool or to stick a new garage in the middle of a new driveway. They are often lucky to afford a coat of paint.

So for both these reasons, our newly formed not-for-profit agency acquired, in 1975, a collection of dilapidated but authentic structures. To be sure, there were leaks and malfunctions aplenty, but no one had painted the structures chartreuse or put in skylights. Sagamore's core buildings were largely as Margaret had left them in 1954.

Many of the camp's farm site and infrastructure buildings, however, were beyond repair. The sugar shack where the Vanderbilt workers had boiled down maple sap for syrup had fallen into its own foundation. The springhouses that fed the 100,000-gallon reservoir had fallen to their knees. The hydroelectric plant, a brick structure, was standing, but its machinery had been pillaged and the dam was broken. Sluice runs were visible but overrun by weeds. The deer pen was a few yards of rusted wire strung on rotten posts. Farm buildings were discernible only by their footprints. All trees of any size around the farm site had been cut for timber by Syracuse University and dragged out on sledges, leaving deep cuts in the meadow soil and damaging the integrity of the farm site. Only a watering trough was left behind to testify to the original Durant and Vanderbilt use.

In all, about thirty buildings, all outside the core of twenty-seven buildings that make up the guest area and the workers' complex, were gone by the mid-'70s. The outlying buildings located on the opposite shore of the lake, on a rise to the south of camp, and those on the outlet were on land purchased by the State of New York to be added to the Forest Preserve. The Forest Preserve is the nomenclature used for land owned by the state within the "Blue Line" or boundary of the Adirondack Park, which includes both public (state-owned) and private lands. As part of "Forever Wild" property—that is, property protected under Article 14 of the New York State Constitution—they could only be noted, not conserved. While this seems harsh to many, the mandate of the Department of Environmental Conservation in the Adirondack Park is to preserve land, not structures. Also, the state's purchase of Sagamore's outlying property meant that no one would ever be able to build on it—a plus for a small not-for-profit serendipitously located on what is essentially a private lake.

In 1975, only the thirteen bark-clad buildings that housed the Vanderbilt guests on a point of land jutting into the lake were purchased for $100,000 by the small not-for-profit. The intent of the directors was to use Sagamore as a conference center for humanistic education groups. Summer conferences began by 1976 and volunteer work weekends by 1977. Volunteer service was priceless given the limited resources of the new owners, a constant that still affects the organization. Barbara Glaser relates that she used to walk through the dining hall every morning with a clipboard to take notes from the guests who reported non-functioning toilets, leaking roofs, malfunctioning light switches and the like. These problems were addressed with varying levels of permanence and with youthful enthusiasm. Fairly soon, a caretaker was hired. Fresh paint was cosmetically applied to room walls in the conference building, ragged carpet was removed and some maintenance projects were tackled.

But in 1985, a major crisis needed to be addressed when the sewer system failed. Repair would require digging out and replacing the leach fields, installing a control panel and repairing necessary pipes. Sagamore Institute had to get its first loan to pay for the project. Happily, the new superintendent of buildings and grounds, Bob Heinsler, was now on board. As a former contractor, he understood systems such as the wastewater system he was faced with repairing. Heinsler brought both maintenance and construction experience to Sagamore, and these strengths evolved into the solid preservation policies and procedures that are his forte.

Meanwhile, Sagamore Institute had just completed an enormous political campaign, canvassing to ensure that a statewide referendum called "Save Sagamore" would be passed. By now the directors realized that the other fourteen extant buildings adjacent to the guest property historically used by the workers were critical to the task of maintaining and interpreting Sagamore. Because the ten acres on which these structures were situated had become part of the Forest Preserve, a referendum to all New York voters had to be proposed and passed. It carried. This was a joyous occasion, but it necessitated a purchase of another piece of property to trade into the Forest Preserve as Sagamore traded out the ten acres. This was a complicated process by most measures, but an understood standard operating procedure for those living in the Forest Preserve. The land trade reunited Sagamore's guest and service complexes.

Now Sagamore had twice as many buildings to preserve, including the "new" buildings that had been neglected for a full thirty years and exposed to the ravages of the long Adirondack winters. To be certain that these dire preservation issues would be addressed, the new deed had forty pages of "do's and don'ts" attached to it. The covenant with the Preservation League of New York State, the New York State Department of Environmental Conservation and Sagamore Institute was signed in 1986 ensuring that Sagamore would remain a "compatible neighbor" with the Forest Preserve.

While most of us are familiar with the duties of the state offices of historic preservation, in the Adirondack and the Catskill regions of New York, the Department of Environmental Conservation (DEC) had been the lead agency, trumping the offices that dealt with preservation. Thus, the covenant is complex. Included in the agreement are these legal topics:

1. *Rehabilitation and Restoration,*
2. *Right to Inspect (by the State and the League),*
3. *Public Viewing (summer solstice to autumnal equinox),*
4. *Construction,*
5. *Signs and Lights,*
6. *Agriculture,*
7. *Topographical Changes,*
8. *Refuse and Materials,*
9. *Water and Soil,*
10. *Roadways,*
11. *Vehicles (no snowmobiles, dune buggies, motorcycles),*
12. *Alcohol,*
13. *Separate Ownership (no subdivision),*
14. *Use (as a conference center, museum, lodge, research center without hazardous or toxic materials, X-C ski center, restaurant, arts/crafts studios/galleries, artists/writers retreat, school, college and/or private residence) provided such uses do not interfere with the viewing, are not carried out in such a way so as to accelerate deterioration, or do not compromise the preservation of the camp in accordance with the conditions, covenants, and restrictions set forth in this indenture,*
15. *Maps and Reports,*
16. *Payment of Taxes,*
17. *Insurance (fire, extended coverage, liability),*
18. *Default (State and/or League shall notify Sagamore in writing),*
19. *Right to Cure,*
20. *Indemnification,*
21. *Right of First Refusal,*
22. *Strict Interpretation (the indenture shall forever run with the land),*
23. *No Waiver,*
24. *Notices,*
25. *No Liability (for the State or League),*
26. *Severability,*
27. *Successors and Assigns,*
28. *Amendments.*

This document became the primary directive for Sagamore's preservation projects and operations. The directors asked Crawford and Stearns Architecture of Syracuse to complete a historic structures report for the newly acquired Service Complex. At this point, Howie Kirschenbaum, EdD, and Barbara Glaser, EdD, the original directors of the Sagamore Institute, stepped down to pursue teaching and philanthropic careers. New directors, Beverly Bridger, MLA, and Michael Wilson, PhD, came aboard in 1989.

In accordance with the Schedule for Rehabilitation, the severe deterioration of the buildings in the workers' complex needed to be addressed. Painting and staining immediately began on the barn, carriage house, Hen House and Chalet. But the barn had more problems than paint.

The trustees joked about leaning against it so it would fall over and they would not have to deal with it. But a small state historic preservation grant had been awarded for barn stabilization, and the new directors, Bridger and Wilson, began a successful fundraising campaign for the dollar-to-dollar match. In 1989, all preservation grants were administered by DEC, not historic preservation offices, so the complicated paperwork went through that office. There would be two subsequent grants for the barn to make it useable for the public, but when the first phase of the work was finished, Sagamore had a ribbon-cutting ceremony. Dan Berggren wrote the song "Big Beams" for the celebration.

Janet Null of Argus Architecture and Preservation was the competent architect for the barn project; under her guidance, the barn beams were reinforced and the roof replaced. Since that first project, Janet has led Sagamore for over twenty years through many more roofing and preservation projects. She also took the lead on penning the Conservation Plan and the Conservation Policy, a yearlong conversation with the board, staff and various constituencies using Sagamore, and she was instrumental in completing the historic structures report on the bark-covered buildings in the guest complex. Her insistence on best practices has always served Sagamore well, and her guidance has been deeply appreciated.

The grant for the barn roof was from Environmental Quality Bond Act monies. Two other EQBA grants were awarded, supporting the repair of seven more roofs. The Main Lodge, the boathouse, and the Playhouse were shingled; the shingles on the Main Lodge were the old asbestos style, thus presenting environmental challenges. Removal had to be carefully managed by workers wearing white suits that made them look like spacewalkers. Those shingles, having lasted for fifty to seventy years, were replaced by a thirty-year fire-retardant roof. Other roofs were metal and had to be power scrubbed, primed and painted.

There were so many roofing drawings to be completed that Janet Null found two architecture students to create a full set of measured drawings for all of Sagamore's buildings. The students lived with us a full summer.

Their drawings proved to be of great use in preparing the Conservation Plan, completed in 1993.

Adirondack weather dictates that roofing repair take place during warm weather, but scheduling these extensive projects around an active summer and fall schedule for guests is no small logistical challenge, particularly when many of the guests are children. Staff members during that period are to be complimented on their skills at providing clear directions and controlling traffic, and construction workers share equal credit for their understanding and patient cooperation.

In 1992, another crisis arose. The first bridge (there are three) crossing the outlet and allowing all vehicles to reach Sagamore was condemned. The January thaw brought water levels up to the planking, and a DEC representative who was in the area became so alarmed that he gave twenty-four-hour notice to closure. The director asked for a meeting to point out that there were guests at Sagamore and staff children who needed the bridge to get to school, not to mention the need to keep the bridge open for emergency vehicles that might be called upon to serve any of the three camps in the area. DEC brought the army along to the meeting to determine if a pontoon bridge might be in order. After twenty-four hours, the water had lowered to a less frightening level, but the order to replace the bridge still stood.

Sagamore's business depends on the bridge remaining open, so we took out a loan and footed the bill. The state eventually repaid Sagamore but it was a battle of nearly a decade, ably led by Bernard Melewski, Esq. Unfortunately, after the fiasco with the first bridge, further challenges awaited us: the state condemned the second bridge. As a result, traffic to all area camps was diverted through Sagamore for nearly a year. This second bridge was jointly owned by Sagamore (one-quarter) and the state (three-quarters) because property lines were drawn down the center of the stream and across the center of the bridge. Sagamore gifted its quarter of the bridge to the state after many months of negotiation. The state then accepted its full responsibility and repaired the bridge to the high standards mandated for all state-operated bridges, meaning that eighteen-wheelers and two-decker tour busses could use it with impunity.

Our bridge saga, however, was not yet over. The third bridge was then condemned. Despite Sagamore's long hours of negotiation to try to deed full ownership to the state, the ownership of this third bridge remains fifty/fifty. Condemnation of this third bridge took place a decade after the other bridge negotiations. Recently, its abutments were reinforced with donations from Sagamore's dedicated supporters, resolving the "condemned" status. The bridge has already proven itself by successfully riding out Hurricane Irene. The two bridges now in full state ownership carry the same weight standards as any bridge on the New York State Turnpike, while the third is rated at a seven-ton limit. The decade of bridge repair finally came to a welcome conclusion.

In 1993, Sagamore redrafted its bylaws and was reincorporated under the Department of Education, Museum Division, as a cultural institution, changing its status from its previous designation as a business under the Department of State, where it was originally mistakenly incorporated. This change also acknowledged our ownership of the real estate known as Sagamore and made fundraising for preservation projects more manageable.

In that same year, Sagamore had the good fortune to become the site of a volunteer project for the Niagara Mohawk Power Corporation (NMPC). The NMPC had used Sagamore as the site of a long conference and so knew the needs of the property. Invited to join us for a trial work weekend, this volunteer partnership has happily lasted well over a decade. Their skilled employees have rewired countless outlets, installed emergency lighting, rewired outdoor lampposts, improved service and brought in a new primary line to Sagamore. We believe that without their annual work weekend in June, Sagamore would not have been able to keep up to code and would now be closed for residential programs. Although the corporate name of Niagara Mohawk has been changed to National Grid, they continue to send us outstanding volunteers who do outstanding work. We are deeply grateful.

In 1994, New York State passed a Safe Drinking Water Act. Although our lake had served as a pure source of water for about forty years, all surface water, even if it was not in a location used by boats with motors, was outlawed. Sagamore was faced with the option of filtering the lake water or digging a well. Board president Rich Torkelson, himself a contractor and valued advisor on Sagamore preservation projects, recommended the well option, and the board agreed. Sagamore drilled the first 100 feet utilizing casing to keep the soft soil out of the drill hole and then hit bedrock. The next 278 feet were drilled through solid bedrock. At nearly 400 feet, the water gushed out and was both plentiful and pure. Tested every month, it has never had to be treated. We advise our guests to dump out whatever containers they have with them and fill them with our pure water to take home.

Matching grants for access and for lighting allowed us to open the barn as a visitors' center in 1996. With moveable seating and staging, the barn provides accessible multipurpose space: staff use it twice daily in season to show the introductory slide show to all tourists before they take the guided walking tour, it becomes a dance floor for weekly barn dances and it also functions as a classroom space, auditorium and performance stage. It was completed just in time because the A&E special on the three Durant Great Camps of Raquette Lake, part of their "America's Castles" series, was filmed in 1994 and was aired in the winter of the next year. Our phone rang off the hook with this national coverage that educated the public to the existence of these wilderness estates from the Gilded Age. As a result, our visitor numbers took a leap in the 1996 season.

By 1997, the year of Sagamore's centennial, Michael Wilson had begun to court the National Parks Service, seeking permission for Sagamore to apply for National Historic Landmark status. Applications are accepted by invitation only, and no Great Camp had ever been added to the National Historic Landmark register. With the support of the Preservation League and with the scholarship of Wes Haynes, who wrote the application, Sagamore proudly received Landmark status in 2000. Besides being a point of great pride, Landmark status meant that Sagamore was able to apply for a Save America's Treasures (SAT) grant.

This prestigious, one-time-only grant was awarded in March 2000. The fund had been established by President and Mrs. Bill Clinton as a celebration of the centennial and was earmarked for preservation of the nation's landmarks. Sagamore's project total of $750,000 was funded, and preservation projects were completed within a three-year window. This generous grant allowed Sagamore to address infrastructure at the Main Lodge, reroof Wigwam, rehabilitate the many roofs of the dining hall and kitchen complex and, for the first time in over three decades, make the School House habitable.

The School House project was so complex that Sagamore needed an additional grant for its completion that could support the SAT effort, and in 2001, the grant was awarded. Located in the workers' complex, this was the final building to be addressed under the covenant that had been attached to Sagamore's deed over a decade earlier and that mandated the rehabilitation of all the building in the previously long-neglected workers' complex. Significant repairs not only involved not roofing and a complete infrastructure installation but also addressed the foundation of the School House. It was under stress because the School House is located in a low drainage area. The building was returned to its original use as staff housing. According to history, the structure was outgrown by staff in about 1914, and the larger Chalet was constructed to house the staff. The earlier building was converted to use as a School House for the caretaker's five children.

Perhaps the most appreciated (by returning guests) project under the SAT was the Main Lodge plumbing. It was not surprising that, in 2002, the original 1897 plumbing in the Main Lodge was causing countless problems. Guests could no longer accept it as "quaint." SAT funds enabled Sagamore to replace the old fixtures and completely repair the system. New bathroom fixtures made overnight stays in our most iconic building again an exciting, attractive experience.

The Save America's Treasures award also allowed Sagamore to address concerns about Wigwam. Its complicated roofline harbored ice dams, making a complete reroofing necessary. The famed exterior bark siding was also severely deteriorated. Because siding with bark is a lost art, Sagamore's intrepid architect Janet Null studied the situation with both academic and practical thoroughness. Over the course of two years, she applied test white cedar bark patches to buildings and watched for shrinkage, buckling, cracking and other deterioration over the long winters. Eventually satisfied that she understood the application of this rustic material properly, she taught the construction workers the methodology for applying the sheathing. We are pleased with the results.

The SAT also funded the reroofing of the Dining Hall Complex. This was no small task because this roof covers the dining hall proper, the kitchen, the staff lounge, icehouse, a guest cottage and the covered walkway connecting them. Photographers have immortalized the view of these complicated interconnecting roofs, and it is one of our most popular postcards. The Dining Complex is the center of anyone's stay at Sagamore. Used for all meals, and seen by all tourists, the Dining Hall Complex roof is a maze of angles and valleys. The original dining structure was not large, but it included an attached porch. The first extension doubled the size of the floor plan. The 1924 addition included a long ell and a five-sided bay window structure nearly as large as the original dining area. The kitchen was part of the original structure and the nearby icehouse was later joined to it. The staff lounge became part of the complex, and when the laundry was converted to George Vanderbilt's cottage, it too joined this complicated complex with the addition of a covered walkway.

After the important preservation projects under the SAT were completed, Sagamore turned its attention over the next five years to our educational mission. Several new permanent exhibits were installed in rehabilitated spaces in the workers' complex to help us tell our story to visitors. In the stable portion of the barn, now our popular Visitors' Center, a life-sized Margaret and Alfred Vanderbilt greet tourists, and Margaret's scrapbooks are opened via DVD. A virtual tour and the story of a lady's maid continue to educate visitors in the next room. There are also large exhibits in the main room of the Visitors' Center of the building phases at Sagamore beginning with Durant (1897–1901) and ending with Margaret's most recent structures. Across the road from the barn, the carriage house features both Thomas C. Durant, the scoundrel who founded the Durant railroad fortune, and his son, William West Durant, who was the architect of the camps. One of Sagamore's talented carpenters, Mr. Roblee, is exhibited, as is the rough and colorful Adirondack guide Alva Dunning. Together, these exhibits give a good cross section of Sagamore's historic personalities.

Through generous grant support, Sagamore has worked with Elevation Films to create DVD presentations that give guests an introductory overview of current history, programs and preservation at Sagamore. Mr. Alfred G. Vanderbilt has generously opened his family scrapbooks to the camera and narrated the story of his family's years at Sagamore. We are in his debt.

Folk artists carry on the traditional arts that built the Great Camps. Sagamore is privileged to host traditional artists who demonstrate for tours in summer and who are supported, in part, by a grant from the New York State Council on the Arts. On days when these personable and professional artists are not at Sagamore giving presentations, they appear for tourists via DVD. Another DVD presentation combines the educational and preservation components of our mission. It captures Bob Heinsler, longtime caretaker and preservationist, on film as he walks us through infrastructure, maintenance and preservation projects. This document will be invaluable to future generations who assume the care and preservation of Sagamore. Taken together and constantly expanded to tell our story, the filming projects that Sagamore has been lucky to help create are a recent treasure.

Near the conclusion of one of our DVDs, a young man tells us that you can never be finished with preservation projects. Too true! Although it seems we've just finished our concentration on roofing repair, we constantly return to roofing projects. Maintenance of all of the Sagamore roofs is the most important of all preservation projects, so we will continue to rehabilitate (and in some cases, readdress) both metal and shingle roofs to preserve our buildings for future use. Although this is a daunting prospect, Sagamore staff and board members feel privileged to serve as caretakers of this Great Camp, with the goal of perpetuating superior stewardship of this treasure.

Taking Care of Sagamore Now

B ecause Mrs. Vanderbilt did not leave an endowment for Sagamore, we rely on income to pay the bills for our twenty-seven-building complex and for the salaries of our dedicated staff. Generating revenue is, therefore, a constant focus, requiring an enormous amount of creative programming. Partnerships with organizations of like mind and similar goals are invaluable. For example, Road Scholar, the Boston-based lifelong learning organization formerly known as Elderhostel, whose educational mission is similar to that of Sagamore, is a vital program partner. Several not-for-profit organizations hold annual retreats here. Our award-winning public tour and the donations of devoted members contribute sufficiently so that Sagamore's modest income is able to meet operation expenses. We are constantly looking for appropriate revenue sources, so we remain open to new ideas, but we depend on tried and true partners with similar missions and also on the services of our remarkable volunteers to make ends meet. Because of their size and complexity, preservation projects are always grant-based. The following capsules of information will throw some light on current, successful, operation activities.

THE VOLUNTEER PROGRAM

We cannot talk about preservation without talking about our loyal volunteers. Sagamore holds three annual work weekends in May, June and October. The May and October weekends aim at opening and closing camp, respectively, and the June weekend does special projects. The volunteer work weekend programs were initiated shortly after the guest complex was purchased in the mid-'70s, and they have been annual events ever since. Some of today's crew of volunteers first came to Sagamore with their parents while they were in diapers, and they have grown up loving Sagamore and donating their time and their skills. It is not unusual during these weekends to talk to people who have been coming for over twenty years. Sagamore considers it a unique honor that the ashes of two volunteers and one intern are scattered at Sagamore.

There are plenty of work projects requiring an array of skills. Painting, interior wood panel cleaning and oiling, carpentry of all kinds, window washing, changing storm windows to screens (and vice versa as the season demands), road work, trail work, gardening, dish washing and reorganizing bookcases—all these and more are samples of the necessary projects. In May, volunteers produce an annual *Volunteer Newsletter* to publicize their contributions to the camp.

In addition to these volunteer contributions, Sagamore is the grateful recipient of more specialized assistance from employee volunteers of our local power corporation, National Grid (formerly Niagara Mohawk Power Corporation). As mentioned, for almost two decades, they have come each June to tackle our electrical systems. We cannot give them enough credit.

Ably organized by Bob Heinsler, superintendent of buildings and grounds since 1985, our work weekends, taken together, accomplish as much as we might expect from a much-needed second full-time caretaker. No wonder, then, that our volunteers are the envy of other landmarks and historic sites. We treasure them.

APPROPRIATE USE: PROGRAMS

After Mrs. Vanderbilt donated the camp to Syracuse University, it was used for educational conferences. Different academic departments would book weeks in summer to hold their own meetings. When Sagamore's maintenance

Folk artists enhance the public tours in summer. Rug braiding, chair caning, guide boat building, woodcarving, Adirondack pack basket building and blacksmithing are among the traditional arts presented. Demonstrations are supported in part by the New York State Council on the Arts.

Square-dancing is the Monday night mixer at Inter-generational Grandparents' and Grandchildren's camp sessions each summer. The most important thing to know about "Grands" is that no parents are allowed.

The Main Lodge is iconic. It is considered William West Durant's grandest building.

Since 1897, a fire in the fireplace of the Main Lodge lounge has meant conversation and camaraderie.

A bird's-eye view of Sagamore emphasizes the importance of the land and our place in it. The red buildings in view are part of the workers' complex.

Sagamore Lake embraces the Main Lodge with its pristine waters.

The Boat House is an original Durant building. Enjoying the lake has always been a Sagamore priority.

Finding the city sport of bowling at a wilderness camp is surprising. But remember that bowling is a unisex sport, and Margaret liked to win! These lanes have never experienced frost heave because the workers dug below Raquette Lake's six-foot frost line before they poured the foundation. They understood their environment.

Above: The Workers' Village or Caretaker's Complex was active every day of the year. Workers and their families lived and worked here year-round, some for many years. The Richard Collins family (head caretaker) reared five children here from 1901 to 1924.

Left: The round table is everyone's favorite in the Dining Hall. The bay window was designed by Margaret when she enlarged the hall again in 1924 to accommodate more guests.

The lake mirrors the shore. Spectacular scenery on the land, on the water and in the night sky have always been characteristic of the Great Camp Sagamore guest experience.

Sagamore Lake welcomes your contemplation in a quiet moment.

was deemed too expensive and difficult, Syracuse University divested itself of the property, but the university's ownership of the camp marked its first use as an educational institution.

Acquired in the mid-'70s by a not-for-profit organization called first the Adirondack Humanistic Education Center, then the National Humanistic Education Center and finally renamed Sagamore Institute, the camp immediately began holding educational conferences organized and managed by outside teaching professionals and workshop leaders. This model was similar to the pattern established by Syracuse University; again, Sagamore was being used on a weekly basis in the summer with leaders deciding on their own programs and recruiting their own participants.

In 1980, when the Winter Olympics was held in Lake Placid, Sagamore opened for the season. Guests were bussed the two hours to Placid, hearing an informative narration about Adirondack history and culture while on the bus. They were given tickets to the venues and then bussed back to Sagamore for dinner. In succeeding years, winter programs included cross-country skiing, snowshoeing, tracking, Elderhostels and many kinds of conferences. In the mid-'90s, Sagamore's enormous fuel bills caused the board to eliminate winter operations.

In 1990, the new directors at Sagamore penned an appropriate historic camp mission "to foster understanding, care, and respect for nature, people and their critical interdependence." The mission invited analysis of the individual's relationship to nature currently and historically. Do we see nature as recreational or inspirational? Is it meant for resource extraction? Can we sustain it? Are we meant to conquer it? Are we meant to protect it? Based on this mission statement, Sagamore inaugurated its own new palette of program choices that dealt with Great Camp history, outdoor skills programs and Adirondack culture, thus replacing the more eclectic array of events offered by entrepreneurial educational contractors. As Sagamore began offering its own programs taught by its own staff faculty, we worked in partnership with Elderhostel (now Road Scholar) to market and conduct classes. One of the programs developed during that period grew rapidly: the intergenerational Grandparents' and Grandchildren's Camp.

GRANDS

Affectionately called "Grands," the intergenerational Grandparents' and Grandchildren's Camp sessions held each summer evolved from ideas that can be credited to Arthur and Carol Kornhaber. A psychiatrist and advocate for grandparents' rights, Arthur lived in the Adirondacks, so he knew of the work of the camp. He approached Sagamore and asked that we try a Sunday through Friday program that would build intergenerational links. There were many factors, he thought, that suggested this model. Not only do many families live at great distances from each other nowadays, but many are also ravaged by divorce, and grandparent visitation rights often become bargaining chips as parents separate. Ties between grandparents and grandchildren would be strengthened, Kornhaber thought, by bringing together these two generations without the parents, and this idea formed the foundation of the program. Sagamore's successful model was the flagship program before the Kornhabers expanded it into Oklahoma and other states. Eventually the founders moved to California, but the model has continued to work at Sagamore. About this time, Elderhostel recognized the value of the "intergenerational" concept and began offering programs that offered everything from seeing the Grand Canyon to visiting Broadway with your grandchild. Over the years, Sagamore's "Grands" grew from a single week to eight weeks of the summer, in partnership with Road Scholar. Sessions have been covered both by *CBS Evening News* and the *Today Show* and have been featured in articles appearing in countless newspapers and magazines.

As a mission-based program, Sagamore's intergenerational camps are now streamlined into three age groupings, each with age-appropriate activities. Each session is divided into moose, bear and deer units to keep them small and "teachable." In broad strokes, outdoor nature discovery and environmental awareness, canoeing and swimming fill the mornings; the afternoons feature music and natural crafts; the evenings host square dances, campfires and a grand finale "creativity" night. The oldest children (eleven- to fourteen-year-olds) refinish a classic cedar canvas canoe each year. For over twenty years, "Grands" has remained Sagamore's most popular program. Last year, a young woman who had attended six years of the camp as a child with her grandmother decided to hold her wedding at Sagamore.

If Mrs. Vanderbilt were here, she might claim the invention of this program because she brought her grandchildren to Sagamore every summer to enjoy many of the same activities on the lake and trails that today's children still enjoy.

THE GREAT OUTDOORS

To stay at Sagamore is to be immersed in the out-of-doors. With both lake and forest surrounding you, with stars overhead at night, with balsam-scented air and the dining hall a walk outside from your cozy room, you are immediately part of the Great Camp experience the moment you leave your car in the lot.

The pristine lake and the miles of trails through the Adirondack Forest Preserve invite exploration. Two programs in partnership with Road Scholar open the season in May and June. Every spring, while mating pairs are in full song and on-territory, we offer Boreal Birding. When the forest flowers bloom, students can enroll for Adirondack Flora, a program that examines several native species of orchids with expert teachers as your guides.

Sagamore's courses bring participants of many ages to experience our world-class natural wonders. Active students from the public sign up for kayaking, canoeing and hiking courses—some geared to women only. Many of these outdoor activities are built regularly into retreats and family events as part of the Great Camp experience. Others are incorporated into our special partnerships such as the Skidmore College Outdoor Orientation Program (SCOOP). Similar programs are offered for several other New York colleges.

Recognizing the importance of the next generation, Sagamore now has an auxiliary for the "under forty" age group. They hold a seat on the board and plan their own active outdoor programs and events. Their input is vital to the future.

ADIRONDACK TRADITIONAL ARTS AND CULTURE

Traditional arts are alive and well at Sagamore. Recreating the folk arts that built the camps, our artists are acknowledged experts. Supported in part by the New York State Council on the Arts, traditional artists enliven our historic workshops every summer with their demonstrations for the tourists. The blacksmith shop's forge rings with the hammer on the anvil for two weeks every summer. Our traditional split-ash pack-basket builder is famous throughout the Adirondacks and has been awarded the Traditional Arts of Upstate New York title of "Adirondack Treasure." The guide boat builder thrills tourists with his stories of this specialized craft that took the "sports" out to hunt and fish. Our woodcarver teaches all age levels, as does our rug braider. Both learned from their grandparents. Quilters have adorned many rooms at Sagamore, and twice yearly they meet here to teach others.

Sagamore's happiest weekend is arguably the Mountain Music and Dance festival over Columbus Day weekend. String band instruments— fiddles, banjos, mandolins, guitars, both lap and hammer dulcimers— are heard throughout camp. Songwriters and singers harmonize, and all performers can expect standing ovations. Classes are for all ages and skill levels.

RETREATS

Visitors to Sagamore quickly learn that cellphone connection is nonexistent here, and there are no television sets. They also realize that the lake and trails are open to them and that time at a campfire is always a good way to spend an evening. As a result, relaxation is assured and camaraderie flourishes. Sagamore is, in every sense of the word, a perfect place for "retreat," as many groups have discovered. The following groups have been coming for several years:

Museumwise is an Upstate New York alliance of museums and historic sites. With a mission of preserving and presenting history, this group is a natural Sagamore partner. Museum directors, educators and curators spend a retreat week each year at Sagamore delving into a variety of topics and chewing on ways to advance and expand the profession.

The New York State Art Teachers Association comes to Sagamore annually so that members can learn from one another and present new techniques for their classrooms. Colleagues take turns presenting techniques that have worked in their classrooms both in and out of doors.

Twice a year, the Creative Healing Connections network offers "Arts and Healing" retreats for women with chronic illnesses. Participants enjoy journaling, sculpture, poetry, song, canoeing and storytelling in the calming environment that Sagamore provides. There are plans, as well, for retreats designed for those with post-traumatic stress disorder.

The newest Sagamore retreat is the Center for Conversation. These weekend events, limited to fewer than twenty participants, begin simply, with a common theme. No lectures are given; everyone contributes to the topic in both one-on-one and whole group discussion. With time to hike, canoe and contemplate, members are able to come back to a topic after a break and delve into it again, often with altered perspective. There is no right answer to these conversations. They are philosophical in nature and depend on active listening as well as informed dialogue.

Great Camps History

In the mid-1990s, the Arts and Entertainment network (A&E) added Durant's three Adirondack camps at Raquette Lake to its "America's Castles" series. This national broadcast educated the public to the existence of these wilderness estates. Uniquely situated to welcome the public for an educational experience, Sagamore relishes its role teaching history and heritage. Sagamore considers its tour to be a two-hour history course.

Over the past thirty years, Sagamore has offered Great Camps courses of various lengths with many qualified instructors. Our current course, in partnership with Road Scholar, is called "The Illusion of Roughing It" and emphasizes the Gilded Age luxury that the Vanderbilts and their guests enjoyed in this remote location. In this course, students see Sagamore in depth, learn why the Great Camps are important to American heritage and enjoy the natural surroundings just as their original owners did.

Sagamore also offers a partnership course called Adirondack Scandals. The course spends time looking at historic facts about the lives and businesses of Cornelius Vanderbilt, Thomas C. Durant, J.P. Morgan, Andrew Carnegie and others who had camps in the Adirondacks. It asks students to discuss their techniques for making money and then the Adirondack connections made possible because of their wealth.

Our students know that history study is always in an exciting state of flux with new books and articles providing new information and, often, asking us to reconsider our intellectual stances. Sagamore is the living embodiment of the nineteenth century's uniquely American exploration of its own attitude toward nature. Why were newly wealthy Gilded Age New Yorkers with every possible privilege, with multiple estates in many locations, both within the United States and abroad, with every luxury, drawn to the Adirondacks? Why undertake the expense of accessing such a remote location, keeping a staff of farm workers, caretakers and artisans year round and imposing modern conveniences like indoor plumbing on the wilderness? Why these elaborate preparations for "roughing it?"

These questions inform the design of all of our educational programs. We note both differences and similarities between the attitudes of the Gilded Age campers and our ideas and attitudes toward nature, and in that way we can explore their reasoning as we discover our own. What did they think compared to what we currently feel about wilderness? Why was it important to them, and why is it meaningful to us? At Sagamore, a National Historic Landmark, we present the camp as the premiere example of the nineteenth century's "wilderness" architectural style, a style developed by William West Durant, carried out by gifted artisans and now recognized as the "rustic." This style depended on nature's own stone and wood spread throughout the Adirondacks as building elements for the mountain retreats that contrasted so clearly to Newport's beach society. In the Adirondacks, campers found natural resources for economic development, as well as a wilderness ripe for recreation and leisure. Durant recognized the possibilities of this new relationship with nature, initially intended for only the wealthy few.

Courses and tours at Great Camp Sagamore embrace these questions.

Historic District

After years of negotiation between our not-for-profit and the State of New York, a new historic district has been approved that will permit and encourage the interpretation of Great Camps as a significant part of our American heritage. The Department of Environmental Conservation has added a new special management area to its State Land Master Plan: the Great Camps Historic District, which surrounds Great Camp Sagamore and Camp Uncas, both now designated National Historic Landmarks. Both these camps were built by William West Durant on contiguous acreage between 1893 and 1897. Durant owned between 600,000 and 1 million acres, and most of it now is protected as State Forest Preserve. Forest Preserve land is divided into several categories including wilderness and wild forest. Sagamore in "wilderness," which was owned by the Vanderbilt family, and Uncas in "wild forest," owned by J.P. Morgan's family, are two miles apart and fall into these separate categories. This means different kinds of educational and recreational activities on and around them were permitted. The wilderness designation does not permit motorized vehicles anywhere; the wild forest designation does permit them on its lakes and trails.

The "historic district" designation was beneficial because both camps are used as educational sites for Sagamore's programs. The process was a long one, but after seven years, the historic district was approved. Now we can concentrate on developing programs that are both educational and recreational. These programs will remind the public that the Great Camps are the manifestation of the nineteenth century's uniquely American romance with nature, a new vision of wilderness as a place for restoration, relaxation and recreation.

One important factor in the evolution of attitudes toward wilderness was the changes that were transforming the essential task of acquiring sufficient food. As cities grew, food was suddenly locally available and no longer had to be grown or hunted by individuals. Now hunting became sport. Now back-to-nature became aesthetic. Now cities, states and the nation began setting aside land as parks. Now, having your own lodge or camp became stylish. Now the rustic was romantic.

To study Durant's accomplishments in the historic district is to look first at his father, Thomas C. Durant, a scoundrel in the railroad business. His management of the Union Pacific during the building of the Transcontinental Railroad is a scandal of enormous proportions, revealed as he added miles of unnecessary track to the route. He created Credit Mobilier, a scandal of enormous proportions involving the Congress and dual payments to Thomas C. Durant for building the eastern portion of the Transcontinental Railroad. Was William West Durant even aware of his father's criminal activity? Or did the son merely do as his father told him and begin developing the Raquette Lake area in good faith for wealthy clients? William West Durant brought steamships for his Blue Mountain and Raquette Lake Steamboat Line and telegraph lines into the woods. He built the shortest standard-gauge railroad in the world to get his clients to his camps. Between 1876 and 1897, he employed over two hundred men and women. He championed the "rustic" style. He cut trees and quarried stone. He built three of his own camps, each with well over twenty buildings, and two churches and he helped oversee other projects for relatives. He built miles of roads and established a post office. He went bankrupt.

As Dr. Michael Wilson tells us in the introduction to Sagamore tours:

> *Durant's wilderness retreats were, of course, no more "camps" than the mansions at fashionable Newport were "cottages." But by devising a plan for the complexes which required going outside to move between sleeping, dining and recreation, by constructing buildings which in their use of stone, bark, and wood are in visual harmony with their woodland settings and which bring the shapes and textures of nature to their interior decor, Durant introduced design innovations in his Adirondack Camps that declared a newly felt affinity with nature. "We humans, and by extension the recreational pursuits enabled by these dwellings, (naturally) belong in this setting," the architecture asserts.*

Sagamore's Main Lodge and guest complex, made famous through the Vanderbilt years of entertaining, have been copied as the "prototypical Great Camp" by the National Park Service for its own lodges and by other architects building in the rustic style, expanding the architecture of nature into every corner of America. Recently Disney adapted "Great Camp" architecture for its Wilderness Lodge in Florida. Sagamore provides a living model for this architectural style, but it contributes far more than an architectural style: it is an exceptional setting to study, learn and experience America's philosophical constructions of the "wilderness ideal." The juxtaposition of an elegant but rustic camp with a very straightforward workers' complex, set out-of-sight, gives unique, extant evidence of the resources required to create the illusion of "roughing it."

Durant's saga is unique. In Raquette Lake, a town of barely one hundred residents, he created three National Historic Landmark sites and left a legacy rich in history and culture. The programs of the historic district will investigate this heritage.

There Is Only One Great Camp Sagamore

U nderstand, please, that when you come to check in, the office staff may be on the back porch looking at the lake because they have heard the loon yodel. The kitchen crew may be viewing a rainbow over Buck, Squirrel and Green Mountains even if there are cookies in the oven. The program leaders will take you hiking with perfect equanimity into a steady rain (because it is only heavy dew) or into a sun-drenched summer morning. The staff knows that program participants will tell them how surprised they are to see stars and how they will always remember that they saw the Milky Way at Sagamore. Tour guides know they will find incredulous visitors on every tour as they learn they can stay in these historic buildings.

Wilderness recreation became popular with the wealthy of the Gilded Age. Like the Arts and Crafts Movement, it was a direct reaction against the industrialization of America. The same men who were bringing railroads and machines to our growing cities were hurrying back to the woods to hunt and fish, albeit in a new luxurious style. There is no doubt that the young William West Durant was modeling his Raquette Lake camps on the country estates of the European aristocracy. They were not just overgrown log cabins à la Abe Lincoln. The American aristocracy became Durant's market.

The idea of hunting and fishing for fun instead of sustenance was at the heart of this innovative recreation. Adding canoeing, croquet, ping-pong and swimming were logical next steps. Technology like plumbing made it possible for the Vanderbilts to live at Sagamore with the same comforts they enjoyed in town.

Keeping Sagamore authentic to this era is not just a matter of covenants on the property. It is the stated purpose of the not-for-profit organization that owns Sagamore. The staff, volunteers and trustees are stewards. We believe in preservation and in using these wonderful buildings for public programs. Other Great Camps are privately held and not accessible or are parts of larger not-for-profits such as colleges and churches. Owners can take buildings down, erect additions or paint the structures chartreuse. Sagamore will remain authentic to the Gilded Age and, as such, will become more and more important as a real and significant historic place.

At Great Camp Sagamore, cellphone service does not exist; grandchildren rush about in freedom; the air is scented with balsam; conversation is a lively art; meals are a community event; imagining the Vanderbilts at play is a hobby; traffic noise doesn't intrude; boreal bird song brightens the dawn; the sound of the brook speaks volumes; campfires are recognized as superior to TV; preservation is a priority; and living history for a few short days as a welcome guest is natural.

This wonderful place, now well past the century mark, still serves admirably as a setting for all our programs and as a magical destination. We believe it will continue to do so if we can continue to maintain and restore it. We are honored by the privilege and awed by the responsibilities of this stewardship.

Our interpretation is based on the way Americans relate to the land, then and now. Why do we camp? What do we really think of the natural world? And what are we teaching our children about it?

You can help preserve Sagamore. Donations are accepted in any amount at Sagamore: Post Office Box 40, Raquette Lake, NY 13436-0040. Thank you.

Richard and Margaret Collins at Sagamore

RECOLLECTIONS FROM THEIR GRANDDAUGHTER,
ELIZABETH COLLINS (D. 2010) WITH THE ASSISTANCE OF
THEIR DAUGHTER, MARGARET COLLINS CUNNINGHAM (D.
2004), AND OTHER FAMILY MEMBERS.

Richard James Collins and Margaret Ellen Callahan were married on October 16, 1901, in Chestertown, New York. They began work as the caretakers of Sagamore when Alfred Vanderbilt bought the camp in January 1902. Sagamore was both home and work until March 1924, when they moved over the ice and by log road to their new home, The Hedges, on Blue Mountain Lake.

Richard was born on November 20, 1872, in North Creek, New York. Raised on a farm near the Hudson River, he ventured farther north as a freight wagon driver on the route from North Creek to Indian Lake and Blue Mountain Lake; he was fourteen when he started. Sometime after that he began working for William West Durant, under the supervision of John Callahan, Margaret's half-brother, who in 1892 had become superintendent of the William West Durant properties in the area south of Raquette Lake.

Margaret was born on July 4, 1868, also in Chestertown. She taught school in Adirondack, New York, and family memory surmises that her summer visits to Raquette Lake provided the opportunity for courtship.

Raising a family while overseeing the growth and operation of Sagamore was both fulfilling and satisfying for the Collins family. Their first home at Sagamore was the apartment over the dining hall and kitchen. After the laundry building (now the conference building) was completed, they moved there. The room that now serves as the director's office was their living room.

The Collins family. Richard Collins was caretaker at Sagamore in the years following Alfred's death.

All five of the Collins children were born while Richard and Margaret were at Sagamore. The first four were born at Saint Elizabeth's Hospital in Utica: John in 1902, Richard in 1904, Patrick in 1906 and Margaret in 1908. Thomas was born on the Collins farm in North Creek in 1910. School, church and town activities were key.

Grade school was easy with classes held right here at Sagamore. But getting to high school presented more of a challenge. John left Sagamore to attend high school in Corinth, New York. The others went each day by wagon or sleigh to the Raquette Lake School. After high school, it was on to Rensselaer Polytechnic Institute, St. Lawrence, Notre Dame and Saint Elizabeth's College in New Jersey.

Each Sunday all of the children, and at least one of their parents, made the trip to Raquette Lake for church, sometimes staying for dinner with Dennis and Mary Dillon. Mary was the daughter of John and Mary Callahan and had been maid-of-honor at Richard and Margaret's wedding. Dennis Dillon, working with Margaret's brother, Maurice, owned and ran the Raquette Lake Supply Company. The Dillon, Callahan and Collins families all had a hand in setting up the Raquette Lake Library. Margaret served on the first board of directors, and Richard was on the school board for many years. Margaret was also active in the Red Cross. Her son, Richard Jr., told of her long hours at a machine that cranked out knitted tubes that were then hand-finished into socks for the soldiers of World War I.

When Richard and Margaret took on the work at Sagamore, John and Mary Callahan were living at Uncas, and Dennis and Libby Lenihan were running Kamp Kill Kare. The family stories are filled with accounts of shared work and shared pleasure. The paint shop at Sagamore was a good place for square dances. Bowling parties, just before the lanes were to be refinished, seem to have been a regular event. Building the toboggan runs at Sagamore and Uncas, and testing them out, was a mutual effort. When the Vanderbilts were in camp in summer, Richard often would take all of the "boys" camping. His daughter Margaret remembers going out for the day with Mrs. Vanderbilt to join the campers for lunch, but she didn't get to stay over.

Mr. and Mrs. Collins shared the work of running the camp. Much of the day-to-day management, such as hiring staff, setting wages and ordering goods and supplies, was done in consultation, generally by mail or telegraph, with the Vanderbilts' secretary, a position held in succession by Messieurs Merriam, Alexander and Crocker. Both also worked directly with Mr. Vanderbilt and then with Mrs. Emerson in planning and executing changes in the camp complex. Richard was always deeply involved in coordinating any construction or renovation. We're told that when the hydroelectric plant was under construction, the engineer proposed that the wires be strung above ground, while Mr. Collins advocated for underground. Arguing that weather could all too easily disrupt services, he persuaded Mr. Vanderbilt to take on the extra time and expense necessary for the underground installation. Mrs. Emerson liked to have Richard take her for a carriage or sleigh ride to look over the camp and to discuss "things." She was especially fond of winter sleigh rides—the snowier the better.

Margaret kept house—on a large scale. She managed the kitchen and housekeeping staff and coordinated the activities of staff that came with the Vanderbilts for large parties or long holidays. The camp was often at capacity over the Christmas holiday. She worked directly with the first Mrs. Vanderbilt, Elsie French, and then with Mrs. Emerson on the purchase and replacement of most of the furnishings.

In 1922, Richard and Margaret Collins bought the Duryea Camp on Blue Mountain Lake. The family memory holds that they simply decided that it was time to have a place of their own. They stayed at Sagamore two more years but, by the summer of 1924, were settled into the operation of the Hedges Hotel, work that would engage them until Richard's death.

Margaret Emerson, My Grandmother—One of a Kind

RECOLLECTIONS FROM HENRY J. TOPPING JR. (D. 2003), MARGARET'S GRANDSON BY HER DAUGHTER GLORIA BAKER

If you didn't know her, she was Mrs. Emerson; but once you met her, a pretty, smiling face with laughing, bright eyes would soon say, "Call me Margaret"—or maybe even "Maggie"—if you wanted to. The staff called her "Madam," but without a hint of servility. My mother, Gloria Mary Baker, called her "Mama," and I called her "Tutu"—Hawaiian for grandmother.

Regardless of how you knew her, who you were or what your relationship with her was, one all-encompassing impression overwhelmed—you had never known anyone quite like her, and you weren't likely to soon again and maybe not ever.

Her respect was not for sale, but it was easily earned. And you wanted to earn it. Good manners and deportment, the kind consideration of others and charity were required to get it. The willingness to learn brought high marks, especially when blended with tolerance and an open mind. She expected a keen sense of fair play on a field of high standards where human frailties were played. Most important, effort was rewarded as much as accomplishment. Both were doubly rewarded.

Her friends and admirers were legion, ranging from heads of state and royalty to shopkeepers and the progeny of slaves, from Broadway composers to prizefighters, from financiers to Cardinals. These friends were unflinchingly loyal. Tutu, you see, was the rare and unmistakable example of all the qualities she prized in others and sought to develop (with some measure of success, I hope) in me. She would invariably point out those esteemed qualities to me—whether they were General George C. Marshall's patriotism and foresight in the Marshall Plan or the charm and wit of the dialogue in George Abbott's plays. Charm and wit are, of course, important ingredients of good humor, and this humor bore an importance of its own.

Tutu inspired others. She brought out their best in people, and they knew it. Important battle strategies were debated by the top navy brass in the seclusion of her Kahala home in Honolulu during World War II. After the war was over, Dick Rogers and Oscar Hammerstein locked themselves up in the house on Banyan Road in Palm Beach to write "Victory at Sea" because they knew they could do it there—having gotten "stuck" everywhere else. Tutu and her hospitality were the common thread of these oddly related but disparate undertakings. (Keeping her young grandson out of the music room was an important component of that hospitality.)

She was a charming, gracious and elegant hostess, constantly entertaining and entertaining constantly. And she loved it. It could have been a black-tie dinner for twenty at her Long Island estate or a whole wild boar barbecue for sixty in the woods at Arcadia, her fourteen-thousand-acre South Carolina plantation. Thus, the redesigning of the Sagamore dining hall to accommodate sixty-five was no accident; it was a self-imposed necessity.

The concept alone might have overwhelmed some, but to her it was simply drawing the plans in the dirt with a stick and asking that it be done in keeping with the rest of Sagamore—while keeping one eagle eye watching. Tutu had what we call in the navy "command presence." This may be roughly defined as the imagination, foresight, power and management skills to create and implement action toward a single end.

It may be that as an only child, even though a girl, she was taught early, whether she liked it or not, by my great-grandfather, Isaac E. Emerson, captain, USNR, Spanish-American War. Certainly, naval tradition—and she was partial to it—carried on in the family as all her male progeny, myself included, served in the navy during times of war.

Or maybe it came from a child- and young-womanhood that included an upbringing in numerous, seriously staffed palatial homes, several round-the-world trips and living abroad, thus developing an incredible sense of planning and logistics. Several full-scale lengthy safaris to Africa in the 1920s could only have helped in that regard.

That the then–Mrs. Vanderbilt would decide to enlarge—rather than abandon—Sagamore, as a thirty-one-year-old mother of two small boys still in her widow's weeds, is not surprising to me. It was probably no more of a challenge to her than teaching Uncle George how to shoot. She was a crack shot, and together—after she taught me—we broke many a clay pigeon off the back porch of the Main Lodge. She was in her fifties then. I recall her sending me throughout various dark passages in the lodge with a .22 rifle to get rid of squirrels. The trout on the dining hall wall attests to her fishing skill. (Fishermen and women, remember how crude the tackle was in those days.)

Here at Sagamore, Tutu orchestrated the running of this Great Camp, meeting the needs of its large staff, which in turn met the needs of the camp; saw to the pleasure and entertainment of a nonstop flow of fifteen to twenty guests, though sometimes many more; and directed the minutiae of her young grandchildren's summers. She did so never missing a beat, pulling it all off with the polish, ease and aplomb of a Toscanini.

Ever cheery, with a quick wink and a smile, she could tell you what and how much was fresh in the garden that day, when the red guide boat would be fixed (wasn't my fault), who was coming next week and why we should take note or that she had arranged for us to go to Old Forge because there was a special movie for children. And she would do all of that between racking her croquet mallet and the game of bocci that was about to begin.

When (and not all that rarely) we were invited to the Main Lodge in the evenings and, if we were good, dinner with the grown-ups, Tutu would be buzzing about—perhaps from a fireplace chat with Baron de Geinsburg, editor of *Vogue* magazine; to the puzzle table where she always seemed to spot that one hard-to-find piece; to the piano, urging her friend Paigie into the current show tunes; to leading me to the newest *National Geographic* with a story she'd just read by Roy Chapman Andrews about the Gobi Desert.

During dinner, this consummately skilled hostess would direct the conversation from geo-politics to local politics—from social conditions to the conditions of "society," the concept of which amused her to no end in its pretentiousness.

The art of conversation was practiced in both its clever and serious forms. But it was never pedantic since the participants were always witty and intelligent and, usually, direct players in the scenarios being discussed. George Abbot would describe current theater and General Marshall would opine about President Truman, Churchill and Stalin, while Uncle Alfred might handicap the Triple Crown.

When I was old enough to understand, I never ceased to be amazed at Tutu's depth and breadth of knowledge, whether arcane or philosophic in content. She was incessantly curious, able to get the best information and intelligent enough to both understand and use it. I truly believe that knowledge meant far more to her than any of her countless possessions.

She was a woman who gave far more than she took, whether it was the cost of a staff person's doctor's bill or the giving of Sagamore itself. And, she did it as inconspicuously as possible. This "head of the Four Hundred," according to the *New York Times* (a title she would have laughed off as a joke), gave discreetly and anonymously. Although unable to escape it, her dislike for publicity was intense.

Tutu's name isn't etched on museum walls. Monuments were not her style. But the families of hundreds (on good source) of American servicemen will never forget that someone they knew only as "someone" had paid to send their sons back to America, all shot up from battle, to recover at home or, unraveled and shell-shocked (post-traumatic stress, today), just to go home to visit. You see, she cared about humanity and the human condition from the lowliest corporal on the Bataan Death March to her friend General Wainright, who marched at the head of his men.

They would all have thanked her if they could, but as she saw it, her deeds bore their own rewards. When told she was being honored for her Red Cross work in the Pacific with America's highest civilian award, she asked if she could receive it in private. With grace, dignity and true humility, she did.

If I had to describe her in a sentence, I'd say that she cared about everyone and everything and that she had a lot of moxie. From economics to politics, the past to the present, the arts to science and from intellect to wit—all these were important. She loved both beauty and sport. Purdy shotguns and Hardy fly rods were as important as stunning diamonds and furs. But being well versed in each skill was more important than any of the trappings. She loved the beauty of the Adirondack woods and the swamps of the Carolina Lowcountry as much as the splendors of the Louvre and the Prado.

She also cared about herself. Her senses of personal pride and dignity were more important to her than social mores or public embarrassment. Adhering to her own high principles, she went to Reno as a young woman and publicly aired family "dirty linen" in order to obtain a justifiable divorce; this was unheard of for women in those days and—though she would arch her eyebrow at me for the phrase—particularly those of her station in life.

Tutu was a God-fearing woman, as they used to say, a Catholic by choice (I say by choice because it was both hers and the church's. Although she married more than once, the church reinstated her for her compelling humanitarianism.) She was, however, ecumenical in her views. She happily numbered Jews, Protestants, Buddhists and Muslims among her friends. Rather than viewing them as heathens or seeking to proselytize, she looked upon them as a source of wisdom.

My grandmother was an extraordinary human being and her life even more so, given her status, the times and the fact that she was a woman. She would probably have made a superb president and, had she done that, a wonderful model for those surely (I hope) to come.

Although it was an accident of birth, no one has come close to her profound influence on my life. Tutu was truly one of a kind.

Selected letters from Mr. Vanderbilt's Secretary Charles Crocker to Richard Collins

Grand Central Station
New York
August 9, 1902

R.J. Collins,
Racquette Lake, N.Y.

Dear Sir:

On September first next, Mr. Edward M. Burns will relinquish his duties as Manager of Sagamore Lodge and Preserve, and beginning with that date, I wish you to take entire charge of the place.

It is my desire to have the property managed as economically as it can be done, compatible with its use, employing as few people as possible for its care and maintenance.

Mr. Burns will turn over to you in due course all his vouchers, blanks, stationery and books of account, which will be written up and balanced to Sept. first, so that you will start on that date with no old outstanding matters to look after.

Render to me promptly between the first and fifth of each month, your accounts for the preceding month, made up in the same form as heretofore, keeping me advised of any unusual developments which may arise.

Yours truly,
Chas. E. Crocker

APPENDIX III

Alfred G. Vanderbilt
358 Fifth Avenue
New York City

December 23, 1907

Mr. R.J. Collins, Supt.,
    Sagamore Lodge
        Racquette Lake, N.Y.

Dear Sir:

A chef and his helper, from Sherry's, will leave here on the day train Thursday for Racquette Lake. Please have some conveyance from Sagamore Lodge meet them on arrival of train.

I do not yet know when Mr. Vanderbilt intends to have the rest of the servants start for Sagamore.

Yours truly,
Chas. E. Crocker
Secretary to
Alfred G. Vanderbilt

Grand Central Station
New York
August 19, 1909

Mr. R.J. Collins,
    Superintendent, Sagamore Preserve,
        Racquette Lake, N.Y.

Dear Sir:

Mr. Vanderbilt says that you may purchase for him, from Mr. Woodruff, ten thousand trout, and have the same put into his lake or streams, in such proportion as you think best. Last year we paid fifty dollars per thousand. I have not heard what Mr. Woodruff will ask for the trout this year.

It would seem as if, with this consignment, the lake would be sufficiently stocked to last for a considerable time. Do you understand that Mr. Woodruff is going to give up his hatchery?

Yours truly,
J.L. Merrimam

Main lodge
steps—Charles
Crocker, Mr.
Vanderbilt's
secretary, and
small Tom
Collins, 1914.
*The Sagamore
collection, courtesy
of H. Collins.*

Alfred G. Vanderbilt
331 Madison Avenue
New York City

January 12, 1915

Mr. R.J. Collins, Supt.,
    "Sagamore Lodge",
        Racquette Lake, N.Y.

Dear Sir:

As per night letter wired to you, a draughtsman from the Bishop Company will come up to-morrow to make a set of plans and measurements of the main lodge; I suppose it will require somewhere about a week. If you want him to make a sketch of the bowling alley building to indicate the measurements required for the curtains, ask him to do so.

Mr. Vanderbilt and I were at the office of the Bishop Company to-day to see preliminary plans for the service building to be about on site of the drying yard, and in connection with discussing matter of hauling materials it was decided to send up two more teams. While at the farm Thursday Mr. Vanderbilt will decide whether to send horses from there of whether 'twill be necessary for him to buy new ones from Lancaster.

Yours truly,
Chas. E. Crocker

Index

Roosevelt, Teddy 18, 24, 25
root cellar 30, 52
rustic style 70, 106, 107

S

Sagamore Lake 31, 38, 61
Sagamore Lodge 15, 17, 121, 122,
    123
School House 90
skeet 53
Smith, Paul 24

T

Twain, Mark 19, 21

U

Uncas 25, 30, 31, 32, 33, 42, 43,
    56, 63, 67, 73, 105, 113

V

Vanderbilt, Alfred 25, 26, 33, 92,
    111
Vanderbilt, Alfred G. 17, 18, 92,
    122
Vanderbilt, Cornelius 25, 35, 36,
    103
Vanderbilt, George 91
Vanderbilt, Reginald 24

W

Wigwam 38, 44, 72, 90, 91
Wilson, Michael 82, 87, 90, 106

Visit us at
www.historypress.net